BC POLICE
TEST PREP

BC Police Entrance Test (JIBC) Study Guide & Practice Test Questions

Copyright © 2020 by Complete Test Preparation Inc. ALL RIGHTS RESERVED. No part of this book may be reproduced or transferred in any form or by any means, graphic, electronic, or mechanical, including photocopying, recording, web distribution, taping, or by any information storage retrieval system, without the written permission of the author.

Notice: Complete Test Preparation Inc. makes every reasonable effort to obtain from reliable sources accurate, complete, and timely information about the tests covered in this book. Nevertheless, changes can be made in the tests or the administration of the tests at any time and Complete Test Preparation Inc. makes no representation or warranty, either expressed or implied as to the accuracy, timeliness, or completeness of the information contained in this book. Complete Test Preparation Inc. makes no representations or warranties of any kind, express or implied, about the completeness, accuracy, reliability, suitability or availability with respect to the information contained in this document for any purpose. Any reliance you place on such information is therefore strictly at your own risk.

The author(s) shall not be liable for any loss incurred as a consequence of the use and application, directly or indirectly, of any information presented in this work. Sold with the understanding, the author(s) is not engaged in rendering professional services or advice. If advice or expert assistance is required, the services of a competent professional should be sought.

The company, product and service names used in this publication are for identification purposes only. All trademarks and registered trademarks are the property of their respective owners. Complete Test Preparation Inc. is not affiliated with any educational institution.

Complete Test Preparation Inc. is not affiliated with any BC Police Service or the Justice Institute of BC, who are not involved in the production of, and do not endorse this publication.

We strongly recommend that students check with exam providers for up-to-date information regarding test content.

Version 9 March 2025

Published by
Complete Test Preparation Inc.
Victoria BC Canada
Visit us on the web at https://www.test-preparation.ca
Printed in the USA
ISBN-13: 9781772454697

About Complete Test Preparation Inc.

Why Us?
The Complete Test Preparation Team has been publishing high quality study materials since 2005, with a catalog of over 145 titles, in English, French and Chinese, as well as ESL curriculum for all levels.

To keep up with the industry changes we update everything all the time!

And the best part?
With every purchase, you're helping people all over the world improve themselves and their education. So thank you in advance for supporting this mission with us! Together, we are truly making a difference in the lives of those often forgotten by the system.

Charities that we support -
https://www.test-preparation.ca/charities-and-non-profits/

You have definitely come to the right place.
If you want to spend your valuable study time where it will help you the most - we've got you covered today and tomorrow.

Feedback

We welcome your feedback. Email us at feedback@test-preparation.ca with your comments and suggestions. We carefully review all suggestions and often incorporate reader suggestions into upcoming versions. As a Print on Demand Publisher, we update our products frequently.

Contents

6 GETTING STARTED
- How this study guide is organized — 7
- The BC Police Study Plan — 8
- Making a Study Schedule — 11

15 READING COMPREHENSION
- Self-Assessment — 16
- Answer Key — 28
- Help with Reading Comprehension — 31
- Main Idea and Supporting Details — 34
- Drawing Inferences And Conclusions — 37
- Drawing Inferences And Conclusions — 38

44 MEMORY
- Self-Assessment — 45
- Memorization and Memory Tricks — 49

52
- Using Mnemonics — 50
- Memory Questions — 55
- Answer Key — 57

58 ENGLISH
- Self-Assessment — 59
- Answer Key — 68
- English Tutorials — 71
- Capitalization — 71
- Colons and Semicolons — 73
- Commas — 74
- Quotation Marks — 77
- Common English Usage Mistakes — 79
- Subject Verb Agreement — 86

93 MATHEMATICS
- Self-Assessment — 97
- Answer Key — 102
- Basic Math Video Tutorials — 107
- Fraction Tips, Tricks and Shortcuts — 107
- Converting Fractions to Decimals — 109

103
    Solving One-Variable Linear Equations 113
    Solving Two-Variable Linear Equations 114
    Adding and Subtracting Polynomials 116
    Multiplying and Dividing Polynomials 117
    Simplifying Polynomials 117
    Factoring Polynomials 118
    Quadratic equations 119
    Percent Tips, Tricks and Shortcuts 121
    Exponents: Tips, Shortcuts & Tricks 123
    Types of Word Problems 128

137 **PRACTICE QUESTIONS SET 1**
    Answer Key 181

201 **PRACTICE QUESTIONS SET 2**
    Answer Key 243

261 **CONCLUSION**

Getting Started

CONGRATULATIONS! By deciding to take the BC Police Police Aptitude Test, you have taken the first step toward a great future! Of course, there is no point in taking this important examination unless you intend to do your best to earn the highest grade you possibly can. That means getting yourself organized and discovering the best approaches, methods and strategies to master the material. Yes, that will require real effort and dedication, but if you are willing to focus your energy and devote the study time necessary, before you know it you will be on your way to a brighter future!

We know that taking on a new endeavour can be scary, and it is easy to feel unsure of where to begin. That's where we come in. This study guide is designed to help you improve your test-taking skills, show you a few tricks of the trade

and increase both your competency and confidence.

The BC Police Aptitude Test

The BC Police has five sections,

- **Reading Comprehension**

- **English** – This section tests your ability to articulate in writing, complex thoughts in a clear and concise way that is understandable to others. This includes, vocabulary, spelling and English grammar.

- **Memory** – Here you are shown a face and asked to choose the same person from four pictures, where their appearance has been altered.

- **Basic Math and Algebra**

While we seek to make our guide as comprehensive as possible, note that like all exams, the BC Police Exam might be adjusted at some future point. New material might be added, or content that is no longer relevant or applicable might be removed. It is always a good idea to give the materials you receive when you register to take the BC Police test a careful review.

How This Study Guide is Organized

This study guide is divided into three sections. The first section, Self-Assessments, will help you recognize your areas of strength and weakness. This will be a boon when it comes to managing your study time most efficiently; there is not much point of focusing on material you have already got firmly under control. Instead, taking the self-assessments will show you where that time could be much better spent. In this area you will begin with a few questions to evaluate quickly your understanding of material that is likely to appear on the BC Police test. If you do poorly in certain areas, simply work carefully through those sections in the tutorials and then try the self-assessment again.

The second section, Tutorials, offers information in each of the content areas, as well as strategies to help you master that material. The tutorials are not intended to be a complete course, but cover general principles. If you find that you do not understand the tutorials, it is recommended that you seek out additional instruction.

Third, we offer two sets of practice test questions, similar to those on the BC Police Exam.

THE BC POLICE STUDY PLAN

Now that you have made the decision to take the BC Police test, it is time to get started. Before you do another thing, you will need to figure out a plan of attack. The very best study tip is to start early! The longer the time period you devote to regular study practice, the more likely you will retain the material and access it quickly. If you thought that 1x20 is the same as 2x10, guess what? It really is not, when it comes to study time. Reviewing material for just an hour per day over the course of 20 days is far better than studying for two hours a day for only 10 days. The more often you revisit a particular piece of information, the better you will know it. Not only will your grasp and understanding be better, but your ability to reach into your brain and quickly and efficiently pull out the tidbit you need, will be greatly enhanced as well.

The great Chinese scholar and philosopher Confucius believed that true knowledge could be defined as knowing what you know and what you do not know. The first step in preparing for the BC Police is to assess your strengths and weaknesses. You may already have an idea of what you know and what you do not know, but evaluating yourself using our Self- Assessment modules for each of the test content areas may surprise you.

Making a Study Schedule

To make your study time the most productive, you will need to develop a study plan. The purpose of the plan is to organize all the bits of pieces of information in such a way that you will not feel overwhelmed. Rome was not built in a day, and learning everything you will need to know to pass the BC Police is going to take time, too. Arranging the material you need to learn into manageable chunks is the best way to go. Each study session should make you feel as though you have reached your goal, and your goal is simply to learn what you planned to learn during that particular session. Try to organize the content in such a way that each study session builds on previous ones. That way, you will retain the information, be better able to access it, and review the previous bits and pieces at the same time.

Self-assessment

The Best Study Tip! The very best study tip is to start early! The longer you study regularly, the more you will retain and 'learn' the material. Studying for 1 hour per day for 20 days is far better than studying for 2 hours for 10 days.

What don't you know?

The first step is to assess your strengths and weaknesses. You may already have an idea of where your weaknesses are, or you can take our Self-assessment modules for each of the content areas.

Exam Component	Rate 1 to 5
Reading Comprehension	
Composition	
Vocabulary	
Spelling	
English Grammar	
Professional Judgment	
Recognition/Identification	
Logic	
Ordering information	
Identifying sequences	
Solving Problems	
Basic Math	
Percent	
Decimals	
Word Problems	

Making a Study Schedule

The key to making a study plan is to divide the material you need to learn into manageable sized pieces and learn it, while at the same time reviewing the material that you already know.

Using the table above, any scores of 3 or below, you need to spend time learning, reviewing and practicing this subject area. A score of 4 means you need to review the material, but you don't have to re-learn it. A score of 5 and you are OK with just an occasional review before the exam.

A score of 0 or 1 means you really need to work on this should allocate the most time and the highest priority. Some students prefer a 5-day plan and others a 10-day plan. It also depends on how much time until the exam.

Here is an example of a 5-day plan based on an example from the table above:

> **Reading Comprehension:** 1- Study 1 hour everyday – review on last day
> **English:** 3 - Study 1 hour for 3 days then ½ hour a day, then review
> **Basic Math:** 4 - Review every second day
> **Memory:** 5 - Review for ½ hour every other day

Using this example, math and memory are good, and only need occasional review. English is good and needs 'some' review. Reading Comprehension is very weak and need most of your time. Based on this, here is a sample study plan:

Day	Subject	Time
Monday		
Study	Reading Comprehension	1 hour
Study	Basic Math	1 hour
½ **hour break**		
Study	English	1 hour
Tuesday		
Study	Reading Comprehension	1 hour
Study	Basic Math	½ hour
½ **hour break**		
Study	English	½ hour
Review	Memory	½ hour
Wednesday		
Study	Reading Comprehension	1 hour
Study	Basic Math	½ hour
½ **hour break**		
Study	English	½ hour
Thursday		
Study	Reading Comprehension	½ hour
Study	Basic Math	½ hour
Review	English	½ hour
½ **hour break**		
Review	Memory	½ hour
Friday		
Review	Reading Comprehension	½ hour
Review	Basic Math	½ hour
Review	English	½ hour

Using this example, adapt the study plan to your own schedule. This schedule assumes 2 ½ - 3 hours available to study everyday for a 5 day period.

First, write out what you need to study and how much. Next figure out how many days before the test. Note, do NOT study on the last day before the test. On the last day before the test, you won't learn anything and will probably only confuse yourself.

Make a table with the days before the test and the number of hours you have available to study each day. We suggest working with 1 hour and ½ hour time slots.

Start filling in the blanks, with the subjects you need to study the most, getting the most time, and the most regular time slots (i.e. everyday) and the subjects that you know getting the least time (e.g. ½ hour every other day, or every 3rd day).

Tips for Making a Schedule

Once you make a schedule, stick with it! Make your study sessions reasonable. If you make a study schedule and don't stick with it, you set yourself up for failure. Instead, schedule study sessions that are a bit shorter and set yourself up for success! Make sure your study sessions are do-able. Studying is hard work, but after you pass, you can party and take a break!

Schedule breaks. Breaks are just as important as study time. Work out a rotation of studying and breaks that works for you.

Build up study time. If you find it hard to sit still and study for 1 hour straight through, build up to it. Start with 20 minutes, and then take a break. Once you get used to 20-minute study sessions, increase the time to 30 minutes. Gradually work you way up to 1 hour.

More on how to study math
https://www.test-preparation.ca/study-math/

How to Study
For more information, see our How to Study Guide at https://www.test-preparation.ca/learning-study/

Flash Cards - The Complete Guide

https://www.test-preparation.ca/flash-cards/

Using your Daily Routine to Study

https://www.test-preparation.ca/daily-routine/

Reading Comprehension

This section contains a self-assessment and reading tutorial. The tutorials are designed to familiarize general principles and the self-assessment contains general questions similar to the reading questions likely to be on the BC Police exam, but are not intended to be identical to the exam questions. The tutorials are not designed to be a complete reading course, and it is assumed that students have some familiarity with reading comprehension and vocabulary questions. If you do not understand parts of the tutorial, or find the tutorial difficult, it is recommended that you seek out additional instruction.

For addition practice and help with reading comprehension see our Multiple Choice Secrets books at www.multiple-choice.ca.

Tour of the Reading Content

Below is a detailed list of the types of reading questions that generally appear on your exam.

- Drawing logical conclusions
- Make predictions
- Analyze and evaluate the use of text structure to solve problems or identify sequences
- Vocabulary - Give the definition of a word from context
- Summarize

The questions below are not the same as you will find on the exam - that would be too easy! And nobody knows what the questions will be and they change all the time. Mostly the changes consist of substituting new questions for old, but the changes can be new question formats or styles, changes to the number of questions in each section, changes to the time limits for each section and combining sections. Below are general reading and vocabulary questions that cover the same areas as the exam. So the format and exact wording of the questions may differ slightly, and change from year to year, if you can answer the questions below, you will have no problem with the reading section.

Reading Comprehension Self-Assessment

The purpose of the self-assessment is:

- Identify your strengths and weaknesses.
- Develop your personalized study plan (above)
- Get accustomed to the BC Police test format
- Extra practice – the self-assessments are almost a full 3rd practice test!
- Provide a baseline score for preparing your study schedule.

Since this is a self-assessment, and depending on how confident you are with reading comprehension and vocabulary, timing is optional. This self-assessment has 15 questions, so allow about 20 minutes to complete this assessment.

Once complete, use the table below to assess your understanding of the content, and prepare your study schedule described in chapter 1.

For more on answering multiple choice in a reading comprehension test, see

https://www.test-preparation.ca/multiple-choice/

80% - 100%	Excellent – you have mastered the content
60 – 79%	Good. You have a working knowledge. Even though you can just pass this section, you may want to review the tutorials and do some extra practice to see if you can improve your mark.
40% - 59%	Below Average. You do not understand reading comprehension problems. Review the tutorials , and retake this quiz again in a few days, before proceeding to the Practice Test Questions.
Less than 40%	Poor. You have a very limited understanding of reading comprehension problems. Please review the tutorials , and retake this quiz again in a few days, before proceeding to the Practice Test Questions.

SELF-ASSESSMENT

	A	B	C	D
1	○	○	○	○
2	○	○	○	○
3	○	○	○	○
4	○	○	○	○
5	○	○	○	○
6	○	○	○	○
7	○	○	○	○
8	○	○	○	○
9	○	○	○	○
10	○	○	○	○
11	○	○	○	○
12	○	○	○	○
13	○	○	○	○
14	○	○	○	○
15	○	○	○	○

Directions: The following questions are based on several reading passages. A series of questions follow each passage. Read each passage carefully, and then answer the questions based on it. You may reread the passage as often as you wish. When you have finished answering the questions based on one passage, go right onto the next passage. Choose the best answer based on the information given and implied.

Questions 1 – 4 refer to the following passage.

Passage 1 - Who Was Anne Frank?

You may have heard mention of the word Holocaust in your History or English classes. The Holocaust took place from 1939-1945. It was an attempt by the Nazi party to purify the human race, by eliminating Jews, Gypsies, Catholics, homosexuals and others they deemed inferior to their "perfect" Aryan race. The Nazis used Concentration Camps, which were sometimes used as Death Camps, to exterminate the people they held in the camps. The saddest fact about the Holocaust was the over one million children under the age of sixteen died in a Nazi concentration camp. Just a few weeks before World War II was over, Anne Frank was one of those children to die.

Before the Nazi party began its persecution of the Jews, Anne Frank had a happy life. She was born in June of 1929. In June of 1942, for her 13th birthday, she was given a simple present which would go onto impact the lives of millions of people around the world. That gift was a small red diary that she called Kitty. This diary was to become Anne's most treasured possession when she and her family hid from the Nazis in a secret annex above her father's office building in Amsterdam.

For 25 months, Anne, her sister Margot, her parents, another family, and an elderly Jewish dentist hid from the Nazis in this tiny annex. They were never permitted to go outside, and their food and supplies were brought to them by Miep

Gies and her husband, who did not believe in the Nazi persecution of the Jews. It was a very difficult life for young Anne and she used Kitty as an outlet to describe her life in hiding. After 2 years, Anne and her family were betrayed and arrested by the Nazis. To this day, nobody is exactly sure who betrayed the Frank family and the other annex residents. Anne, her mother, and her sister were separated from Otto Frank, Anne's father. Then, Anne and Margot were separated from their mother. In March of 1945, Margot Frank died of starvation in a Concentration Camp. A few days later, at the age of 15, Anne Frank died of typhus. Of all the people who hid in the Annex, only Otto Frank survived the Holocaust.

Otto Frank returned to the Annex after World War II. It was there that he found Kitty, filled with Anne's thoughts and feelings about being a persecuted Jewish girl. Otto Frank had Anne's diary published in 1947 and it has remained continuously in print ever since. Today, the diary has been published in over 55 languages and more than 24 million copies have been sold around the world. The Diary of Anne Frank tells the story of a brave young woman who tried to see the good in all people.

1. From the context clues in the passage, what does annex mean?

    a. Attic

    b. Bedroom

    c. Basement

    d. Kitchen

2. Why do you think Anne's diary has been published in 55 languages?

    a. So everyone could understand it.

    b. So people around the world could learn more about the horrors of the Holocaust.

    c. Because Anne was Jewish but hid in Amsterdam and died in Germany.

    d. Because Otto Frank spoke many languages.

3. From the description of Anne and Margot's deaths in the passage, what can we assume typhus is?

    a. The same as starving to death.

    b. An infection the Germans gave to Anne.

    c. A disease Anne caught in the concentration camp.

    d. Poison gas used by the Germans to kill Anne.

4. In the third paragraph, what does outlet mean?

    a. A place to plug things into the wall

    b. A store where Miep bought cheap supplies for the Frank family

    c. A hiding space similar to an Annex

    d. A place where Anne could express her private thoughts.

Questions 5 – 8 refer to the following passage.

Passage 2 - Was Dr. Seuss A Real Doctor?

A favorite author for over 100 years, Theodor Seuss Geisel was born on March 2, 1902. Today, we celebrate the birthday of the famous "Dr. Seuss" by hosting Read Across America events throughout the March. School children around the country celebrate the "Doctor's" birthday by making hats, giving presentations and holding read aloud circles featuring some of Dr. Seuss' most famous books.

But who was Dr. Seuss? Did he go to medical school? Where was his office? You may be surprised to know that Theodor Seuss Geisel was not a medical doctor at all. He took on the nickname Dr. Seuss when he became a noted children's book author. He earned the nickname because people said his books were "as good as medicine." All these years later, his nickname has lasted and he is known as Dr. Seuss all across the world.

Think back to when you were a young child. Did you ever want to try "green eggs and ham?" Did you try to "Hop on Pop?" Do you remember learning about the environment from a creature called The Lorax? Of course, you must recall one of Seuss' most famous characters; that green Grinch who stole Christmas. These stories were all written by Dr. Seuss and featured his signature rhyming words and letters. They also featured made up words to enhance his rhyme scheme and even though many of his characters were made up, they sure seem real to us today.

And what of his "signature" book, The Cat in the Hat? You must remember that cat and Thing One and Thing Two from your childhood. Did you know that in the early 1950's there was a growing concern in America that children were not becoming avid readers? This was, book publishers thought, because children found books dull and uninteresting. An intelligent publisher sent Dr. Seuss a book of words that he thought all children should learn as young readers. Dr. Seuss wrote his famous story The Cat in the Hat, using those words. We can see, over the decades, just how much influence his writing has had on very young children. That is why we celebrate this doctor's birthday each March.

5. What does the word "avid" mean in the last paragraph?

    a. Good

    b. Interested

    c. Slow

    d. Fast

6. What can we infer from the statement "His books were like medicine?"

    a. His books made people feel better

    b. His books were in doctor's office waiting rooms

    c. His books took away fevers

    d. His books left a funny taste in readers' mouths.

7. Why is the publisher in the last paragraph called "intelligent?"

a. The publisher knew how to read.

b. The publisher knew that kids did not like to read.

c. The publisher knew Dr. Seuss would be able to create a book that sold well.

d. The publisher knew that Dr. Seuss would be able to write a book that would get young children interested in reading.

8. The theme of this passage is

a. Dr. Seuss was not a doctor.

b. Dr. Seuss influenced the lives of generations of young children.

c. Dr. Seuss wrote rhyming books.

d. Dr. Suess' birthday is a good day to read a book.

Questions 9 - 12 refer to the following passage.

Keeping Tropical Fish

Keeping tropical fish at home or in your office used to be very popular. Today, interest has declined, but it remains as rewarding and relaxing a hobby as ever. Ask any tropical fish hobbyist, and you will hear how soothing and relaxing watching colorful fish live their lives in the aquarium. If you are considering keeping tropical fish as pets, here is a list of basic equipment you will need.

A filter is essential for keeping your aquarium clean and your fish alive and healthy. There are different types and sizes of filters and the right size for you depends on the size of the aquarium and the level of stocking. Generally, you need a filter with a 3 to 5 times turn over rate per hour. This means that the water in the tank should go through the filter about 3 to 5 times per hour.

Most tropical fish do well in water temperatures ranging between 24^0 C and 26^0 C, though each has its own ideal water temperature. A heater with a thermostat is necessary to regulate the water temperature. Some heaters are submersible and others are not, so check carefully before you buy.

Lights are also necessary, and come in a large variety of types, strengths and sizes. A light source is necessary for plants in the tank to photosynthesize and give the tank a more attractive appearance. Even if you plan to use plastic plants, the fish still require light, although here you can use a lower strength light source.

A hood is necessary to keep dust, dirt and unwanted materials out of the tank. Sometimes the hood can also help prevent evaporation. Another requirement is aquarium gravel. This will improve the aesthetics of the aquarium and is necessary if you plan to have real plants.

9. What is the general tone of this article?

    a. Formal

    b. Informal

    c. Technical

    d. Opinion

10. Which of the following cannot be inferred?

    a. Gravel is good for aquarium plants.

    b. Fewer people have aquariums in their office than at home.

    c. The larger the tank, the larger the filter required.

    d. None of the above.

11. What evidence does the author provide to support their claim that aquarium lights are necessary?

   a. Plants require light.

   b. Fish and plants require light.

   c. The author does not provide evidence for this statement.

   d. Aquarium lights make the aquarium more attractive.

12. Which of the following is an opinion?

   a. Filter with a 3 to 5 times turn over rate per hour are required.

   b. Aquarium gravel improves the aesthetics of the aquarium.

   c. An aquarium hood keeps dust, dirt and unwanted materials out of the tank.

   d. Each type of tropical fish has its own ideal water temperature.

Questions 13 - 16 refer to the following passage.

The Civil War

The Civil War began on April 12, 1861. The first shots of the Civil War were fired in Fort Sumter, South Carolina. Note that even though more American lives were lost in the Civil War than in any other war, not one person died on that first day. The war began because eleven Southern states seceded from the Union and tried to start their own government, The Confederate States of America.

Why did the states secede? The issue of slavery was a primary cause of the Civil War. The eleven southern states relied heavily on their slaves to foster their farming and plantation lifestyles. The northern states, many of whom had already abolished slavery, did not feel that the southern states should have slaves. The north wanted to free all the slaves and President Lincoln's goal was to both end slavery and preserve the Union. He had Congress declare war on the Confederacy on April 14, 1862. For four long, blood soaked years, the North and South fought.

From 1861 to mid 1863, it seemed as if the South would win this war. However, on July 1, 1863, an epic three day battle was waged on a field in Gettysburg, Pennsylvania. Gettysburg is remembered for being the bloodiest battle in American history. At the end of the three days, the North turned the tide of the war in their favor. The North then went on to dominate the South for the remainder of the war. Another famous event is General Sherman's "March to The Sea," where he famously led the Union Army through Georgia and the Carolinas, burning and destroying everything in their path.

In 1865, the Union army invaded and captured the Confederate capital of Richmond Virginia. Robert E. Lee, leader of the Confederacy surrendered to General Ulysses S. Grant, leader of the Union forces, on April 9, 1865. The Civil War was over and the Union was preserved.

13. What does secede mean?

    a. To break away from

    b. To accomplish

    c. To join

    d. To lose

14. Which of the following statements summarizes a FACT from the passage?

   a. Congress declared war and then the Battle of Fort Sumter began.

   b. Congress declared war after shots were fired at Fort Sumter.

   c. President Lincoln was pro slavery

   d. President Lincoln was at Fort Sumter with Congress

15. Which event finally led the Confederacy to surrender?

   a. The battle of Gettysburg

   b. The battle of Bull Run

   c. The invasion of the confederate capital of Richmond

   d. Sherman's March to the Sea

16. What does the word abolish as used in this passage mean?

   a. To ban

   b. To polish

   c. To support

   d. To destroy

Answer Key

1. A
We know that an annex is like an attic because the text states the annex was above Otto Frank's building.

Choice B is incorrect because an office building doesn't have bedrooms. Choice C is incorrect because a basement would be below the office building. Choice D is incorrect because there would not be a kitchen in an office building.

2. B
The diary has been published in 55 languages so people all over the world can learn about Anne. That is why the passage says it has been continuously in print.

Choice A is incorrect because it is too vague. Choice C is incorrect because it was published after Anne died and she did not write in all three languages. Choice D is incorrect because the passage does not give us any information about what languages Otto Frank spoke.

3. C
Use the process of elimination to figure this out.

Choice A cannot be the correct answer because otherwise, the passage would have simply said that Anne and Margot both died of starvation. Choices B and D cannot be correct because, if the Germans had done something specifically to murder Anne, the passage would have stated that directly. By the process of elimination, choice C has to be the correct answer.

4. D
We can figure this out using context clues. The paragraph is talking about Anne's diary and so, outlet in this instance is a place where Anne can pour her feelings.

Choice A is incorrect answer. That is the literal meaning of the word outlet and the passage is using the figurative meaning. Choice B is incorrect because that is the secondary literal meaning of the word outlet, as in an outlet mall. Again, we are looking for figurative meaning. Choice C is incorrect because there are no clues in the text to support that answer.

5. B
When someone is avid about something that means they are highly interested in the subject. The context clues are dull and boring, because they define the opposite of avid.

6. A
The author is using a simile to compare the books to medicine. Medicine is what you take when you want to feel better. They are suggesting that if you want to feel good, they should read Dr. Seuss' books.

Choice B is incorrect because there is no mention of a doctor's office. Choice C is incorrect because it is using the literal meaning of medicine and the author is using medicine in a figurative way. Choice D is incorrect because it makes no sense. We know not to eat books.

7. D
The publisher is described as intelligent because he knew to get in touch with a famous author to develop a book that children would be interested in reading.

Choice A is incorrect because we can assume that all book publishers must know how to read. Choice B is incorrect because it says in the article that more than one publisher was concerned whether children liked to read. Choice D is incorrect because there is no mention in the article about how well The Cat in the Hat sold when it was first published.

8. B
The passage describes in detail how Dr. Seuss had a great effect on the lives of children through his writing. It names several of his books, tells how he helped children become avid readers and explains his style of writing.

Choice A is incorrect because that is just one single fact about the passage. Choice C is incorrect because that is just one single fact about the passage. Choice D is incorrect because that is just one single fact about the passage. Again, choice B is correct because it encompasses ALL the facts in the passage, not just one single fact.

9. B
The general tone is informal.

10. B
The statement, "Fewer people have aquariums in their office than at home," cannot be inferred from this article.

11. B
Light is necessary for the fish and plants.

12. B
The following statement is an opinion, " Aquarium gravel improves the aesthetics of the aquarium."

13. A
Secede means to break away from because the 11 states wanted to leave the United States and form their own country.

Choice B is incorrect because the states were not accomplishing anything. Choice C is incorrect because the states were trying to leave the USA not join it. Choice D is incorrect because the states seceded before they lost the war.

14. B
Look at the dates in the passage. The shots were fired on April 12 and Congress declared war on April 14.

Choice C is incorrect because the passage states that Lincoln was against slavery. Choice D is incorrect because it never mentions who was or was not at Fort Sumter.

15. C
The passage states that Lee surrendered to Grant after the capture of the capital of the Confederacy, which is Richmond.

Choice A is incorrect because the war continued for 2 years after Gettysburg. Choice B is incorrect because that battle is not mentioned in the passage. Choice D is incorrect because the capture of the capital occurred after the march to the sea.

16. A
When the passage said that the North had *abolished* slavery, it implies that slaves were no longer allowed in the North. In essence slavery was banned.

Choice B makes no sense relative to the context of the passage. Choice C is incorrect because we know the North was fighting slavery, not for it. Choice D is incorrect because slavery is not a tangible thing that can be destroyed. It is a practice that had to be outlawed or banned.

Help with Reading Comprehension

At first sight, reading comprehension tests look challenging especially if you are given long essays to answer only two to three questions. While reading, you might notice your attention wandering, or you may feel sleepy. Do not be discouraged because there are various tactics and long range strategies that make comprehending even long, boring essays easier.

Your friends before your foes. It is always best to tackle essays or passages with familiar subjects rather than those with unfamiliar ones. This approach applies the same logic as tackling easy questions before hard ones. Skip passages that do not interest you and leave them for later when there is more time.

Don't use 'special' reading techniques. This is not the time for speed-reading or anything like that – just plain ordinary reading – not too slow and not too fast.

Read through the entire passage and the questions before you do anything. Many students try reading the questions first and then looking for answers in the passage thinking this approach is more efficient. What these students do not realize is that it is often hard to navigate in unfamiliar roads. If you do not familiarize yourself with the passage first, looking for answers become not only time-consuming but also dangerous because you might miss the context of the answer you are looking for. If you read the questions first you will only confuse yourself and lose valuable time.

Familiarize yourself with reading comprehension questions. If you are familiar with the common types of reading questions, you are able to take note of important parts of the passage, saving time. There are six major kinds of reading questions.

- **Main Idea**- Questions that ask for the central thought or significance of the passage.

- **Specific Details** - Questions that asks for explicitly stated ideas.

- **Drawing Inferences** - Questions that ask for a statement's intended meaning.

- **Context Meaning** – Questions that ask for the meaning of a word depending on the context.

Read. Read. Read. The best preparation for reading comprehension tests is always to read, read and read. If you are not used to reading lengthy passages, you will probably lose concentration. Increase your attention span by making a habit out of reading.

Reading Comprehension tests become less daunting when you have trained yourself to read and understand fast. Always remember that it is easier to understand passages you are interested in. Do not read through passages hastily. Make mental notes of ideas that you think might be asked.

Reading Strategy

When facing the reading comprehension section of a standardized test, you need a strategy to be successful. You want to keep several steps in mind:

- **First, make a note of the time and the number of sections.** Time your work accordingly. Typically, four to five minutes per section is sufficient. Second, read the directions for each selection thoroughly before beginning (and listen well to any additional verbal instructions, as they will often clarify obscure or confusing written guidelines). You must know exactly how to do what you're about to do!

- **Now you're ready to begin reading the selection.** Read the passage carefully, noting significant characters or events on a scratch sheet of paper or underlining on the test sheet. Many students find making a basic list in the margins helpful. Quickly jot down or underline one-word summaries of characters, notable happenings, numbers, or key ideas. This will help you better retain information and focus wandering thoughts. Remember, however, that your main goal in doing this is to find the information that answers the questions. Even if you find the passage interesting, remember your goal and work fast but stay on track.

- Now read the question and all of the choices. Now you have read the passage, have a general idea of the main ideas, and have marked the important points. Read the question and all of the choices. Never choose an answer without reading them all! Questions are often designed to confuse – stay focused and clear. Usually the answer choices will focus on one or two facts or inferences from the passage. Keep these clear in your mind.

- **Search for the answer.** With a very general idea of what the different choices are, go back to the passage and scan for the relevant information. Watch for big words, unusual or unique words. These make your job easier as you can scan the text for the particular word.

- Mark the Answer. Now you have the key information that the question is looking for. Go back to the question, quickly scan the choices and mark the correct one.

Understand and practice the different types of standardized reading comprehension tests. See the list above for the different types. Typically, there will be several questions dealing with facts from the selection, a couple more inference questions dealing with logical consequences of those facts, and periodically an application-oriented question surfaces to force you to make connections with what you already know. Some students prefer to answer the questions as listed, and feel classifying the question and then ordering is wasting precious time. Other students prefer to answer the different types of questions in order of how easy or difficult they are. The choice is yours and do whatever works for you. If you want to try answering in order of difficulty, here is a recommended order, answer fact questions first; they're easily found within the passage. Tackle inference problems next, after re-reading the question(s) as many times as you need to. Application or 'best guess' questions usually take the longest, so save them for last.

Use the practice tests to try out both ways of answering and see what works for you.

For more help with reading comprehension, see Multiple Choice Secrets at www.multiple-choice.ca

Main Idea and Supporting Details

Identifying the main idea, topic and supporting details in a passage can feel like an overwhelming task. The passages used for standardized tests can be boring and seem difficult - Test writers don't use interesting passages or ones that talk about things most people are familiar with. Despite these obstacles, all passages and paragraphs will have the information you need to answer the questions.

The topic of a passage or paragraph is its subject. It's the general idea and can be summed up in a word or short phrase. On some standardized tests, there is a short description of the passage if it's taken from a longer work. Make sure you read the description as it might state the topic of the passage. If not, read the passage and ask yourself, "Who or what is this about?" For example:

> Over the years, school uniforms have been hotly debated. Arguments are made that students have the right to show individuality and express themselves by choosing their own clothes. However, this brings up social and academic issues. Some kids cannot afford to wear the clothes they like and might be bullied by the "better dressed" students. With attention drawn to clothes and the individual, students will lose focus on class work and the reason they are in school. School uniforms should be mandatory.

Ask: What is this paragraph about?

Topic: school uniforms

Once you have the topic, it's easier to find the main idea. The main idea is a specific statement telling what the writer wants you to understand about the topic. Writers usually state the main idea as a thesis statement. If you're looking for the main idea of a single paragraph, the main idea is called the topic sentence and will probably be the first or last sentence. If you're looking for the main idea of an entire passage, look for the thesis statement in either the first or last paragraph. The main idea is usually restated in the conclusion. To find the main idea of a passage or paragraph, follow these steps:

1. Find the topic.

2. Ask yourself, "What point is the author trying to make about the topic?"

3. Create your own sentence summarizing the author's point.

4. Look in the text for the sentence closest in meaning to yours.

Look at the example paragraph again. It's already established that the topic of the paragraph is school uniforms. What is the main idea/topic sentence?

Ask: "What point is the author trying to make about school uniforms?"

Summary: Students should wear school uniforms.

Topic sentence: School uniforms should be mandatory.

Main Idea: School uniforms should be mandatory.

Each paragraph offers supporting details to explain the main idea. The details could be facts or reasons, but they will always answer a question about the main idea. What? Where? Why? When? How? How much/many? Look at the example paragraph again. You'll notice that more than one sentence answers a question about the main idea. These are the supporting details.

Main Idea: School uniforms should be mandatory.

Ask: Why? Some kids cannot afford to wear clothes they like and could be bullied by the "better dressed" kids. Supporting Detail

With attention drawn to clothes and the individual, Students will lose focus on class work and the reason they are in school (Supporting Detail).

What if the author doesn't state the main idea in a topic sentence? The passage will have an implied main idea. It's not as difficult to find as it might seem. Paragraphs are always organized around ideas. To find an implied main idea, you need to know the topic and then find the relationship between the supporting details. Ask yourself, "What is the point the author is making about the relationship between the details?"

> Cocoa is what makes chocolate good for you. Chocolate comes in many varieties. These delectable flavors include milk chocolate, dark chocolate, semi-sweet, and white chocolate.

Ask: What is this paragraph about?

Topic: Chocolate

Ask: What? Where? Why? When? How? How much/many?

Supporting details: Chocolate is good for you because it is made of cocoa, Chocolate is delicious, Chocolate comes in different delicious flavors

Ask: What is the relationship between the details and what is the author's point?

Main Idea: Chocolate is good because it is healthy and it tastes good.

Drawing Inferences And Conclusions

Drawing inferences and making conclusions happens all the time. In fact, you probably do it every time you read—sometimes without even realizing it! For example, remember the first time that you saw the movie "The Lion King." When you meet Scar for the first time, he is trapping a helpless mouse with his sharp claws preparing to eat it. When you see this action you guess that Scar is going to be a bad character in the movie. Nothing appeared to tell you this. No caption came across the bottom of the screen that said "Bad Guy." No red arrow pointed to Scar and said "Evil Lion." No, you made an inference about his character based on the context clue you were given. You do the same thing when you read!

When you draw an inference or make a conclusion you are doing the same thing, you are making an educated guess based on the hints the author gives you. We call these hints "context clues." Scar trapping the innocent mouse is the context clue about Scar's character.

Usually you are making inferences and drawing conclusions the entire time that you are reading. Whether you realize it or not, you are constantly making educated guesses based on context clues. Think about a time you were reading a book and something happened that you were expecting to happen. You're not psychic! Actually, you were picking up on the context clues and making inferences about what was going to happen next!

Let's try an easy example. Read the following sentences and answer the questions at the end of the passage.

Shelly really likes to help people. She loves her job because she gets to help people every single day. However, Shelly has to work long hours and she can get called in the middle of the night for emergencies. She wears a white lab coat at work and usually she carries a stethoscope.

Video Tutorial

https://www.test-preparation.ca/making-inferences/

Drawing Inferences And Conclusions

Drawing inferences and making conclusions happens all the time. In fact, you probably do it every time you read—sometimes without even realizing it! For example, remember the first time you saw the movie "The Lion King." When you meet Scar for the first time, he is trapping a helpless mouse with his sharp claws preparing to eat it. When you see this action you guess that Scar is going to be a bad character in the movie. Nothing appeared to tell you this. No caption came across the bottom of the screen that said "Bad Guy." No red arrow pointed to Scar and said "Evil Lion." No, you made an inference about his character based on the context clue you were given. You do the same thing when you read!

When you draw an inference or make a conclusion you are doing the same thing, you are making an educated guess based on the hints the author gives you. We call these hints "context clues." Scar trapping the innocent mouse is the context clue about Scar's character.

Usually you are making inferences and drawing conclusions the entire time that you are reading. Whether you realize it or not, you are constantly making educated guesses based on context clues. Think about a time you were reading a book and something happened that you were expecting to happen. You're not psychic! Actually, you were picking up on the context clues and making inferences about what was going to happen next!

Let's try an easy example. Read the following sentences and answer the questions at the end of the passage.

Shelly really likes to help people. She loves her job because she gets to help people every single day. However, Shelly has to work long hours and she can get called in the middle of the night for emergencies. She wears a white lab coat at work and usually she carries a stethoscope.

What is most likely Shelly's job?

    a. Musician
    b. Lawyer
    c. Doctor
    d. Teacher

This probably seemed easy. Drawing inferences isn't always this simple, but it is the same basic principle. How did you know Shelly was a doctor? She helps people, she works long hours, she wears a white lab coat, and she gets called in for emergencies at night. Context Clues! Nowhere in the paragraph did it say Shelly was a doctor, but you were able to draw that conclusion based on the information provided in the paragraph. This is how it's done!

There is a catch, though. Remember that when you draw inferences based on reading, you should only use the information given to you by the author. Sometimes it is easy for us to make conclusions based on knowledge that is already in our mind—but that can lead you to drawing an incorrect inference. For example, let's pretend there is a bully at your school named Brent. Now let's say you read a story and the main character's name is Brent. You could NOT infer that the character in the story is a bully just because his name is Brent. You should only use the information given to you by the author to avoid drawing the wrong conclusion.

Let's try another example. Read the passage below and answer the question.

Social media is an extremely popular new form of connecting and communicating over the Internet. Since Facebook's original launch in 2004, millions of people have joined in the social media craze. In fact, it is estimated that almost 75% of all Internet users aged 18 and older use some form of social media. Facebook started at Harvard University as a way to get students connected. However, it quickly grew into a worldwide phenomenon and today, the founder of Facebook, Mark Zuckerberg has an estimated net worth of 28.5 billion dollars.

Facebook is not the only social media platform, though. Other sites such as Twitter, Instagram, and Snapchat have since been invented and are quickly becoming just as popular! Many social media users actually use more than one type of social media. Furthermore, most social media sites have created mobile apps that allow people to connect via social media virtually anywhere in the world!

What is the most likely reason that other social media sites like Twitter and Instagram were created?

a. Professors at Harvard University made it a class project.

b. Facebook was extremely popular and other people thought they could also be successful by designing social media sites.

c. Facebook was not connecting enough people.

d. Mark Zuckerberg paid people to invent new social media sites because he wanted lots of competition.

Here, the correct answer is B. Facebook was extremely popular and other people thought they could also be successful by designing social media sites. How do we know this? What are the context clues? Take a look at the first paragraph. What do we know based on this paragraph? Well, one sentence refers to Facebook's original launch. This suggests that Facebook was one of the first social media sites. In addition, we know that the founder of Facebook has been extremely successful and is worth billions of dollars. From this we can infer that other people wanted to imitate Facebook's idea and become just as successful as Mark Zuckerberg.

Let's go through the other answers. If you chose A, it might be because Facebook started at Harvard University, so you drew the conclusion that all other social media sites were also started at Harvard University. However, there is no mention of class projects, professors, or students designing social media. So there doesn't seem to be enough support for choice A.

If you chose C, you might have been drawing your own conclusions based on outside information. Maybe none of your friends are on Facebook, so you made an inference that Facebook didn't connect enough people, so more sites were invented. Or maybe you think the people who connect on Facebook are too old, so you don't think Facebook connects enough people your age. This might be true, but remember inferences should be drawn from the information the author gives you!

If you chose D, you might be using the information that Mark Zuckerberg is worth over 28 billion dollars. It would be easy for him to pay others to design new sites, but remember, you need to use context clues! He is very wealthy, but that statement was giving you information about how successful Facebook was—not suggesting that he paid others to design more sites!

So remember, drawing inferences and conclusions is simply about using the information you are given to make an educated guess. You do this every single day so don't let this concept scare you. Look for the context clues, make sure they support your claim, and you'll be able to make accurate inferences and conclusions!

Testing Tips for Main Idea Questions

1. Skim the questions – not the answer choices - before reading the passage.

2. Questions about main idea might use the words "theme," "generalization," or "purpose."

3. Save questions about the main idea for last. Sometimes, the answers to the rest of the questions can be found in order in the passage.

3. Underline topic sentences in the passage. Most tests allow you to write in your test booklet.

4. Answer the question in your own words before looking at the answer choices. Then match your answer with an answer choice.

5. Cross out incorrect answer choices immediately to prevent confusion.

6. If two of the answer choices mean the same thing but use different words, they are BOTH incorrect.

7. If a question asks about the whole passage, cross out the answer choices that apply only to part of it.

8. If only part of the information is correct, that answer choice is incorrect.

9. An answer choice that is too broad is incorrect. All information needs to be backed up by the passage.

10. Answer choices with extreme wording are usually incorrect.

Memory

This section contains a self-assessment questions and tutorials. The tutorials are designed to familiarize general principles and the self-assessment contains general questions similar to the questions likely to be on the exam, but are not intended to be identical to the exam questions. If you do not understand parts of the tutorial, or find the tutorial difficult, it is recommended that you seek out additional instruction.

The questions in the self-assessment are not the same as you will find on the exam - that would be too easy! And nobody knows what the questions will be and they change all the time. Mostly, the changes consist of substituting new questions for old, but the changes also can be new question formats or styles, changes to the number of questions in each section, changes to the time limits for each section, and combining sections. So the format and exact wording of the questions may differ slightly, and changes from year to year, if you can answer the questions below, you will have no problem with the questions on the BC Police Entrance Exam.

Memory Self-Assessment

Directions: You have five minutes to memorize the following information. Do not write anything down. Questions follow the tutorials (page 55).

Name: Angela Jones
Description: 5 ft. 2 in. Black Canadian with long frizzy hair. No other identifying features.

Wanted For: Fraud

Name: Ryan McPherson
Description: 5 ft 8 in. Brown hair, clean-cut. Earring in right ear.

Wanted For: Bank Robbery

Make/Model: Unknown
Color: Red
License Plate: AJ1 26K British Columbia
Wanted in Connection with: Armed Robbery

Make/Model: Chevrolet Impala
Color: Yellow
License Plate: ARU-8364 Alberta
Wanted in Connection with: Assault

Name: Mike Johnson
Description: 5 ft. 8 in Short hair and clean-cut. No other identifying features.

Wanted For: Trafficking

Name: Bryson Strong
Description: 5 ft. 5 in Short hair and clean cut. Scar on left forehead.

Wanted For: Drunk and Disorderly

Make/Model: Mini Cooper
Color: 2-tone Turquoise and White
License Plate: AMCR-834 Ontario
Wanted in Connection with: Vehicular Homicide

Make/Model: Peugeot Coupe
Color: Green
License Plate: A52 BCP Quebec
Wanted in Connection with: Stolen Vehicle

Memorization and Memory Tricks

If you are going to master the art of studying, you are going to have to master one of life's basic skills: memorization. Do not panic! It is not as hard as you might think. Learning a few basic memorization techniques will give you the skills you need to make learning and retaining information a cinch.

Repeat, Repeat, Repeat. Repetition is a clever way of convincing your brain that the material you are studying is important. That is because, when an idea, a person, or an event is important to you, your mind will return to it again and again. By constantly and consistently reviewing new material, you will lock in the facts that you need to remember. Put simply, repetition saturates your brain with facts, words, and ideas to the point that you can't help but remember them later when you need them for a test.

Say It Out Loud. Verbalizing the information that you are studying is another way to embed it into your mind. Speaking the words aloud is like a double repetition, because you are simultaneously speaking them and hearing them. This involves your brain in yet another way, increasing the likelihood that you will remember the facts when you need them. As well, saying the words aloud actually teaches your mouth to recognize them. When you are trying to recall the information and can remember a phrase, whispering it tonics yourself can bring the entire piece of information right back into your mind.

Make Connections. Humor is a useful tool to help you memorize a fact that just isn't sticking. Instead of looking at the information logically and intellectually, consider it in terms of associations or images. For example, let's say you are trying to learn the definition of 'scoliosis.' The word means curvature of the spine. You might notice that the letter 's' occurs three times, and that this letter is a curvy one. It is also the first letter in the word 'spine.' When you see the word on a test, you will recognize the curving letters and remember the association with 'spine!'

When you create a strange association, your brain sees this as something out of the ordinary. The brain has a sense of humor, and enjoys making puns, putting together unusual images and, otherwise having fun with language and ideas. It remembers things that are out of the ordinary more than it does the commonplace. So the more bizarre that you make this combination, the better your chance of recalling the information.

Keep in mind that using only one of these suggestions in and of itself is not the ultimate key to memorization. If a technique doesn't work for a particular bit of information, try another. You can even combine a couple of approaches. The more you use these strategies, the more likely your brain will agree with you that the material you are studying is not only worth remembering, it is actually enjoyable.

Below are some additional strategies to help you memorize material. Try different ones and see what sticks the best for you.

Using Mnemonics

Mnemonics are tricks to help you remember information. Mnemonics come in several varieties, allowing you to choose what clicks for you. Some mnemonics enjoy widespread use because they are easy and effective, but you can always make up your own.

Visual Mnemonics– Visual mnemonics involve creating images that somehow suggest the information that is to be remembered. The image might be connected to the information in some logical way, or it can be completely unrelated. For example, if you are trying to remember that an event took place in Chillicothe, Ohio, you could visualize a cup of coffee sitting in a freezer (chilly coffee). Imaging a map of the state of Ohio on the coffee much will to help you in remembering that Chillicothe is in Ohio.

Visual mnemonics can be useful in learning another language as well. For example, rey is the Spanish word for king or monarch. Visualizing a crown with rays of light coming out from it reinforces the meaning with a mental image. The Spanish verb caminar means 'to walk,' so you could visualize an old El Camino model of car that is broken down, forcing you to walk.

Acronyms – Acronyms use the letters in a phrase or sentence to create an easy-to-remember word. A well-known example of this is ROY G. BIV. The letters stand for red, orange, yellow, green, blue, indigo and violet, which are the colors of the spectrum in order. This technique can be combined with a visual mnemonic to further lock it in. Imagining a cartoon character names Roy G. BIV, who wears a red hat, has orange hair, a yellow tie, a green shirt, a blue belt, indigo pants and a violet shirt makes the information you are trying to memorize impossible to forget!

A variation of the acronym mnemonic is to use the letters to create a simple sentence. With the spectrum colors, 'Richard of York Gave Battle in Vain' can serve as a memory device. Creating a simple song to go along with a sentence mnemonic makes remembering the words a tad easier.

Here is an example for anyone who is studying biology and needs to know taxonomy classifications. By looking at the first letters of each word in the acronym 'Kids Prefer Cheese Over Fried Green Spinach,' it is easy to remember Kingdom, Phylum, Class, Order, Family, Genus, Species, and these are the taxonomy classifications in order.

Acronyms can be used for any subject, including math. For example, at first glance pi seems like a hopelessly long string of numbers that is nearly impossible to memorize. However, the acronym 'How I wish I could calculate pi' is all you need to know. Here, the acronym isn't based on the first letter of each word, but on the number of letters in each word. The first word, 'how' has three letters. 'I' is a single letter, while 'wish' is a four-letter word. These are the first 3 numbers in pi—3.14. The number of letters in each word represents one digit of pi, giving you 3.141592. Memorizing a simple, fun phrase can save a lot of time and brain power.

Taking a Mnemonic Journey – Also known as the Method of Loci, journey mnemonics simply involve taking a mental journey with the information you are trying to integrate.
As you study, imagine yourself walking through a familiar area. Picture words or images that represent the information superimposed on or featured in a particular location along the journey. For example, if you are studying art history, you might imagine yourself walking through your home, from the entrance to the bedroom. Throughout your walk, visualize famous paintings or sculptures along the walls, floor, or in the doorways. Take the mental walk a few times to really lock in the information. By mentally retracing those steps during the art history exam, the art work and artists will be easy to recall.

This method does not have to be used with paintings, sculptures or other obviously visual items. You can combine it with one or more other techniques and apply them to any subject. Picturing something in a specific location that you know well will help reinforce the connection. For example, the crown with rays of light coming out of it may be hanging on your bedpost, while the El Camino is parked outside your window.

Word Play – Rhymes and catchy phrases are an excellent mnemonic approach for adults as well as for children. They do not have to be complicated and can be used for any subject. Some rhymes have been so ingrained in us that decades after learning them, they come back to help us remember how to spell a word or recall a fact. Remembering the spelling mnemonic, 'I before E, except after C, or when sounded like A, as in neighbor and weigh,' has helped many a child—and adult--manage difficult spelling challenges. Remembering the meanings of the homonyms 'there,' 'their,' and 'they're' is made easier by recalling the catchy phrase, 'Here' is in 'there', 'heir' is in 'their', and they're just means they are. This works because both 'here' and 'there' are locations, while 'their' refers to possession, and an 'heir' inherits possessions. You can create a little rhyme to explain all kinds of words you have trouble remembering how to spell. For example, 'There are three e's buried in the cemetery' helps unblock confusion about which vowel to use.

Associations – Another way to remember something is to associate the information with something easier to recall. While associations can be loosely grouped with other types of mnemonics, they are actually a little different. For example, many people have difficulty remembering the difference between stalactites and stalagmites. Stalactites grow down from the cave's ceiling, and there is a 'c' in the middle of the word. Stalagmites, however, contains a 'g', and since they grow up from the ground, that 'g' can stand for 'ground.' Confusing dessert and desert is a very common mistake, but it is easy to create an association to help you remember the difference. For example, the Sahara is a famous desert, and both words contain a single 's.' Another word for dessert is sweets, and both of those words contain two letters 's.'

Associations do not have to be based on spelling. For a physical example on how associations can work, take a look at your hands. You are going to use the knuckles and the spaces between them as association points to the months in the year. Starting with your left pinky knuckle, name the months. The months that fall in the spaces between the knuckles have 30 days, except for February. Those that land on the knuckles are months can contain 31 days. For this trick to work, skip the valley between thumb and index fingers and jump to the right hand's index knuckle, since July and August have 31 days. Another physical mnemonic useful for teaching youngsters how to remember which is their right hand and which the left involves forming an 'L' with the thumb and index finger of the left hand. The 'L' is going in the correct direction, so that is the left hand.

Memory tricks can make studying easier process, regardless of your age. They do not have to be logical, sensible or even related to your subject, and your favorites may not work for other people. The trick is to make sure the mnemonics you use are ones that work for you.

How to Memorize - The Complete Guide
https://www.test-preparation.ca/memorize/

Memory

	A	B	C	D
1	○	○	○	○
2	○	○	○	○
3	○	○	○	○
4	○	○	○	○
5	○	○	○	○
6	○	○	○	○

Memory Questions

1. What is the name of the African Canadian wanted for fraud?

    a. Ryan McPherson

    b. Angela Jones

    c. Bryson Strong

    d. Mike Johnson

2. What Province is the car wanted in connection with armed robbery from?

    a. Alberta
    b. Quebec

    c. British Columbia

    d. Ontario

3. What model is the Chevrolet from Alberta?

    a. Impala

    b. Malibu

    c. Caprice

    d. Lumina

4. Who is wanted for trafficking?

    a. Bryson Strong
    b. Mike Johnson
    c. Angela Jones

    d. Ryan McPherson

5. What is the Mini Cooper wanted for?

    a. Stolen vehicle
    b. Vehicular homicide
    c. Armed Robbery
    d. Assault

6. What Province is the Peugeot Coupe from?

    a. Alberta
    b. Quebec
    c. British Columbia
    d. Ontario

Answer Key

1. B
Angela Jones is the Black Canadian.

2. C
The red car, unknown model and make wanted for armed robbery is from British Columbia.

3. A
The Chevrolet model is an Impala.

4. B
Mike Johnson is wanted for trafficking.

5. B
The Mini Cooper is wanted in connection with a vehicular homicide.

6. B
The Peugeot Coupe is from Quebec.

ENGLISH

THIS SECTION CONTAINS A SELF-ASSESSMENT. The tutorials are designed to familiarize general principles and the self-assessment contains general questions similar to the composition questions likely to be on the exam, but are not intended to be identical to the exam questions. The tutorials are not designed to be a complete course, and it is assumed that students have some familiarity with English grammar and usage. If you do not understand parts of the tutorial, or find the tutorial difficult, it is recommended that you seek out additional instruction.

TOUR OF THE ENGLISH CONTENT

Below is a detailed list of the topics likely to appear on the exam.

- Spelling

- Vocabulary

- English usage

- English grammar

The questions in the self-assessment are not the same as you will find on the exam - that would be too easy! And nobody knows what the questions will be and they change all the time. Mostly, the changes consist of substituting new questions for old, but the changes also can be new question formats or styles, changes to the number of questions in each section, changes to the time limits for each section, and combining sections. So the format and exact wording of the questions may differ slightly, and changes from year to year, if you can answer the questions below, you will have no problem with the Composition section.

English Self-Assessment

The purpose of the self-assessment is:

- Identify your strengths and weaknesses.
- Develop your personalized study plan (above)
- Get accustomed to the format
- Extra practice – the self-assessments are almost a full 3rd practice test!
- Provide a baseline score for preparing your study schedule.

Since this is a Self-assessment, and depending on how confident you are with composition, timing yourself is optional. This self-assessment has 60 questions, so allow 30 minutes to complete.

Answer Sheet

	A	B	C	D	E			A	B	C	D	E
1	○	○	○	○	○		21	○	○	○	○	○
2	○	○	○	○	○		22	○	○	○	○	○
3	○	○	○	○	○		23	○	○	○	○	○
4	○	○	○	○	○		24	○	○	○	○	○
5	○	○	○	○	○		25	○	○	○	○	○
6	○	○	○	○	○		26	○	○	○	○	○
7	○	○	○	○	○		27	○	○	○	○	○
8	○	○	○	○	○		28	○	○	○	○	○
9	○	○	○	○	○		29	○	○	○	○	○
10	○	○	○	○	○		30	○	○	○	○	○
11	○	○	○	○	○							
12	○	○	○	○	○							
13	○	○	○	○	○							
14	○	○	○	○	○							
15	○	○	○	○	○							
16	○	○	○	○	○							
17	○	○	○	○	○							
18	○	○	○	○	○							
19	○	○	○	○	○							
20	○	○	○	○	○							

Fill in the Blanks

1. Our _____ to America by sea was not very comfortable.

    a. journey
    b. voyage
    c. travel
    d. none of the above

2. I do not want to _____ a friend like you.

    a. lose
    b. loose
    c. lost
    d. none of the above

3. This pain killer will _____ your pain.

    a. lesson
    b. lessen
    c. lesen
    d. leson

4. Collecting stamps, _____ and listening to shortwave radio were Rick's main hobbies.

    a. building models
    b. to build models
    c. having built models
    d. build models

Directions: Choose the correct version of the underlined word or phrase in the given sentence.

5. She is the <u>most cleverest</u> girl in the class.

    a. She is the most clever girl in the class.

    b. She is the cleverest girl in the class.

    c. She is the most cleverer girl in the class.

    d. None of the above.

6. He <u>lived</u> in California since 1995.

    a. He had lived in California since 1995.

    b. He has been living in California since 1995.

    c. He has living in California since 1995.

    d. None of the above.

7. Politics <u>are</u> his chief interest.

    a. Politics is his chief interest.

    b. Politics are his chief interests.

    c. Politics is his chief interests.

    d. The sentence is correct.

8. He is a <u>cowered</u> person.

    a. He is a cowardest person.

    b. He is a cowardly person.

    c. He is a coward person.

    d. The sentence is correct.

9. Choose the sentence with the correct grammar.

a. The man was asked to come with his daughter and her test results.

b. The man was asked to come with her daughter and her test results.

c. The man was asked to come with her daughter and our test results.

d. None of the above.

10. Choose the sentence with the correct grammar.

a. Neither of them came with their bicycle.

b. Neither of them came with his bicycle.

c. Neither of them came with our bicycle.

d. None of the above.

11. Choose the correct spelling.

a. Weather

b. Weathur

c. Wether

d. None of the above

12. Choose the correct spelling.

a. Withdrawl

b. Withdrawal

c. Withdrawel

d. Witdrawal

13. Choose the correct spelling.

    a. Yatch

    b. Yache

    c. Yaute

    d. Yacht

14. Choose the correct spelling.

    a. Yeild

    b. Yielde

    c. Yield

    d. Yeelde

15. Choose the correct spelling.

    a. Warrant

    b. Warrent

    c. Warent

    d. Warant

16. Choose the correct spelling.

    a. Thorou

    b. Thurough

    c. Thorough

    d. Thorogh

17. Choose the correct spelling.

    a. Tomorow

    b. Tomorrow

    c. Tommorow

    d. Tommorrow

18. Choose the correct spelling.

    a. Unicke

    b. Uniqe

    c. Unique

    d. None of the Above

19. Choose the correct spelling.

    a. Unice

    b. Usable

    c. Ussable

    d. Usabble

20. Choose the correct spelling.

    a. Usually

    b. Usualy

    c. Ususally

    d. Ussually

Fill in the Blank.

21. When Joe broke his _____ in a skiing accident, his entire leg was in a cast.

    a. Ankle

    b. Humerus

    c. Wrist

    d. Femur

22. Alan had to learn the _____ system of numbering when his family moved to Great Britain.

   a. American
   b. Decimal
   c. Metric
   d. Fingers and toes

23. After Lisa's aunt had her tenth child, Lisa found that she had more than twenty _____.

   a. Uncles
   b. Friends
   c. Stepsisters
   d. Cousins

24. She was a rabid Red Sox fan, attending every game, and demonstrating her _____ by cheering more loudly than anyone else.

   a. Knowledge
   b. Boredom
   c. Commitment
   d. Enthusiasm

25. When Craig's dog was struck by a car, he rushed his pet to the _____.

   a. Emergency room
   b. Doctor
   c. Veterinarian
   d. Podiatrist

26. Gasoline is very _____.

    a. Volatile

    b. Flammable

    c. Inert

    d. None of the above

27. The tree has _____ over millions of years.

    a. Scared

    b. Petrified

    c. Rotted

    d. None of the above

28. They always get along and never _____.

    a. Bicker

    b. Socialize

    c. Debate

    d. None of the above

29. Her reputation as a _____ often gets her into trouble.

    a. Maverick

    b. Conformist

    c. Insider

    d. None of the above

30. Don't worry it will _____ in a few minutes.

    a. Degenerate

    b. Dissipate

    c. Scatter

    d. None of the above

Answer Key

1. B
"Travel" is a verb meaning to go from one place to another. A "journey" is a noun that refers to the travel event. A "voyage" is a journey by sea.

2. A
"Lose" is a verb meaning to misplace something or to fail at a competition. "Loose" is an adjective meaning untied or able to move freely.

3. B
"Lessen" means to reduce in size or intensity. "Lesson" refers to a formal time period in which particular information is taught or learned.

4. A
Present progressive "building models" is correct in this sentence.

5. B
Cleverest is the proper form to express 'most clever.'

6. B
Past perfect continuous, has been living, is proper because the time element, since 1995, and he is still living there now.

7. A
In spite of the 's' ending, "politics" is a singular noun.

8. B
"Cowardly" is an adjective used to modify a person.

9. A
A Pronoun should conform to its antecedent in gender, number and person.

10. B
Words such as neither, each, many, either, every, everyone, everybody and any should take a singular pronoun. Here

we are assuming the subject is male, and so use "his." The subject could be female, in which case we would use "her," however that is not one of the choices here.

11. A
Weather is the correct spelling.

12. B
Withdrawal is the correct spelling.

13. D
Yacht is the correct spelling.

14. C
Yield is the correct spelling.

15. A
Warrant is the correct spelling.

16. C
Thorough is the correct spelling.

17. B
Tomorrow is the correct spelling.

18. C
Unique is the correct spelling.

19. B
Usable is the correct spelling.

20. A
Usually is the correct spelling.

21. D
Femur NOUN the bone of the thigh or upper hind limb, articulating at the hip and the knee.

22. C
Metric System NOUN the decimal measuring system based on the meter, litre, and gram as units of length, capacity, and weight or mass.

23. D
Cousin NOUN a child of one's uncle or aunt.

24. D
Enthusiasm NOUN intense and eager enjoyment, interest, or approval.

25. C
Veterinarian NOUN a person qualified to treat diseased or injured animals.

26. A
Volatile Adjective ordinary, dull; everyday; unexceptional. (2) a person walking along a road or in a developed area.

27. B
Petrified ADJECTIVE changed to stone

28. A
Bicker VERB to quarrel in a tiresome, insulting manner.

29. A
Maverick NOUN showing independence in thoughts or actions.

30. B
Dissipate VERB to disperse or scatter.

English Grammar and Punctuation Tutorials

Capitalization

Although many of the rules for capitalization are pretty straight forward, there are several tricky points that are important to review.

Starting a Sentence

Everyone knows that you need to capitalize the first letter of the first word in a sentence, but is it really all that easy to figure out where one sentence starts and another stops? Take these three examples:

That was the moment it really sunk in: There would be no hockey this year.

It was April and that could mean only one thing: baseball.

We played for hours before heading home; everyone felt tired and happy.

In the first example, the first letter after the colon is capitalized, while in the second example it is not. That is because everything after the first example's colon is a complete sentence, while after example two's colon there is only one word. In example three you have what could be a complete sentence ("everyone felt tired and happy"), but which is not because it follows a semicolon, making it just another clause instead.

Within a sentence you can have an additional complete sentence if the sentence follows a colon. However, if what could be a complete sentence follows a semicolon, it is a clause, and is not capitalized.

Remember that the same rules apply for quotation marks

that apply for colons: A complete sentence inside quotation marks is capitalized, but a single word or phrase is not.

Proper Nouns

The first letter of all proper nouns needs to be capitalized. There are many categories of proper noun. The most common proper nouns are specific names of people (such as Bill), places (such as Germany) or things (such as Honda Civic). However, there are several less obvious categories of words that should be capitalized as proper nouns.

Historical events such as World War II or the California Gold Rush need to be capitalized.

The names of celestial bodies such as Orion's Belt need to be capitalized.

The names of ethnicities such as African-American or Hispanic need to be capitalized.

Relationship words that replace a person's name such as Mom, Doctor and Mister need to be capitalized. However, this only happens when you use the word to replace the person's name. In the sentence, "My mom went to the store," you do not capitalize it, while in the sentence, "Hey Mom, did you get toothpaste at the store?" you do capitalize it.

Geographical locations are capitalized. This can get a little tricky because capitalized geographical locations and non-capitalized directions are easy to confuse. Saying, "We drove south for hours," is a direction, so the word "south" should not be capitalized. However, when saying, "While in the United States, we drove to the South to look at Civil War battle fields," you do capitalize the word "South." The difference is that in the first sentence "south" is just the direction you drove. In the second sentence "the South" is a specific region of the United States that formed itself into the Confederacy during the US Civil War.

Proper Adjectives

Proper adjectives are the adjective forms of proper nouns. People from Germany are German; people from Canada are Canadian. German and Canadian are proper adjectives because they are forms of proper nouns that are used to describe other nouns.

Titles of Works

Titles of works are generally capitalized following a specific pattern. Capitalize all of the important words in a sentence. Do not capitalize unimportant words such as prepositions and articles.

For example: Alien Spaceship Spotted over Many of the World's Capitals

Notice that the prepositions "over" and "of," and the article "the" are the only non-capitalized words in the sentence.

Colons and Semicolons

Within a sentence there are several different types of punctuation marks that can denote a pause. Each of these punctuation marks has different rules when it comes to its structure and usage, so we will look at each one in turn.

Colons

The colon is used primarily to introduce information. It can start lists such as in the sentence, "There were several things Susan had to get at the store: bread, cereal, lettuce and tomatoes." Or a colon points out specific information, such as in the sentence, "It was only then that the group fully realized what had happened: The Martian invasion had begun."

Note that if the information after the colon is a complete sentence, you capitalize and punctuate it exactly like you would a sentence. If, however, it does not constitute a complete sentence, you don't have to capitalize anything. ("Peering out the window Meredith saw them: zombies.")

SEMICOLONS

Semicolons aresuper commas. They denote a stronger stop than a comma does, but they are still weaker than a period, not quite capable of ending a sentence. Semicolons are primarily used to separate independent clauses that are not being separated by a coordinating conjunction. ("Chris went to the store; he bought chips and salsa.") Semicolons can only do this, however, when the ideas in each clause are related. For instance, the sentence, "It's raining outside; my sister went to the movies," is not a proper usage of the semicolon since those clauses have nothing to do with each other.

Semicolons can also be used in lists if more element in the list is itself made up of a smaller list. If you want to write a list of things you plan to bring to a picnic, and those things only include a Frisbee, a chair and some pasta salad, you would not need to use a semicolon. But if you also wanted to bring plastic knives, forks and spoons, you would need to write your sentence like this: "For our picnic I am bringing a Frisbee; a chair; plastic knives, forks and spoons; and some pasta salad."

Using semicolons like this preserves the smaller list that you have in your larger list.

COMMAS

Commas are probably the most commonly used punctuation mark in English. Commas can break the flow of writing to give it a more natural sounding style, and they are the main punctuation mark used to separate ideas. Commas also separate lists, introductory adverbs, introductory prepositional phrases, dates and addresses.

The most rigid way that commas are used is when separating clauses. There are two primary types of clauses in a sentence, independent and subordinate (sometimes called dependent). Independent clauses are clauses that express a complete thought, such as, "Tim went to the store." Subordinate clauses, on the other hand, only express partial thoughts that expand on an independent clause, such as, "after the game ended," which you can see is clearly not a complete sentence. (You will learn more about clauses in different lessons.)

The rule for commas with clauses is that a comma must separate the clauses when a subordinate clause comes first in a sentence: "After the game ended, Tim went to the store." But there should not be a comma when a subordinate clause follows an independent clause: "Tim went to the store after the game ended." If you leave the comma out of the first example, you have a run-on sentence. If you add one into the second example, you have a comma-splice error. Also, when you have two independent clauses joined with a coordinating conjunction, you need to separate them with a comma. "Tim went to the store, and Beth went home."

There are some artistic exceptions to these rules, such as adding a pause for literary effect, but for the most part, they are set in stone.

Commas are also used to separate items in a list. This area of English is unfortunately less clear than it should be, with two separate rules depending on what standard you are following. To understand the two different rules, let's pretend you are having a party at your house, and you are making a list of refreshments your friends will want. You may decide to serve three things: 1) pizza 2) chips 3) drinks. There are two different rules governing how you should punctuate this. According to many grammar books, you would write this as, "At the store I will buy pizza, chips, and drinks."

This variation puts a comma after each item in the list. It is the version that the style books used in most college English and history courses will prefer, so it is probably the one you should follow. However, the Associated Press style guide, which is used in college journalism classes and at newspapers and magazines, says the sentence should be written like this: "At the store I will buy pizza, chips and drinks."

Here you only use a comma between the first two words, letting the word "and" act as the separator between the last two.

Another important place to use commas is when you have a modifier that describes an element of a sentence, but that does not directly follow the thing it describes. Look at the sentence: "Tim went over to visit Beth, watching the full moon along the way." In this sentence there is no confusion about who is "watching the full moon"; it is Tim, probably as he walks to Beth's house. If you remove the comma, however, you get this: "Tim went over to visit Beth watching the full moon along the way." Now it sounds as though Beth is watching the full moon, and we are forced to wonder what "way" the moon is traveling along.

Commas are also used when adding introductory prepositional phrases and introductory adverbs to sentences. A comma is always needed following an introductory adverb. ("Quickly, Jody ran to the car.") Commas are even necessary when you have an adverb introducing a clause within a sentence, even if the clause not the first clause of the sentence. ("Amanda wanted to go to the movie; however, she knew her homework was more important.")

With introductory prepositional phrases you only add a comma if the phrase (or if a group of introductory phrases) is five or more words long. Thus, the sentence you just read did not have a comma following its introductory prepositional phrase ("With introductory prepositional phrases") because it was only four words. Compare that to this sentence with a five word introductory phrase: "After the ridiculously long class, the friends needed to relax."

The last way commas are used in sentences is to separate information that does not need to be there. For instance, "My cousin Hector, who wore a blue hat at the party, thought you were funny." The fact that Hector wore a blue hat is interesting, but it is not vital to the sentence; it could be removed and not changed the sentence's meaning. Therefore, it gets commas around it. Along these lines you should remember that any clause introduced by the word that is considered to provide essential information to the sentence and should not get commas around it. Conversely, any clause starting with the word which is considered nonessential and should not get commas around it.

Quotation Marks

Quotation marks are used in English in a variety of different ways. The most common use of quotation marks is to show quotations either, as dialogue or, when directly quoting a source in an essay or news article. Fortunately, both of these uses follow the same basic rules.

When you have a quote written as the second part of a sentence, you need to put a comma before the quotation marks and a period inside the quotation marks at the end. (Franklin said, "Let's go to the store.") Conversely, when you have quote as the first part of the sentence with information describing it second, a comma replaces the period at the end of the sentence inside the quotes. ("Let's go to the store," Franklin said.)

If the information in a quote is not a complete sentence, you do not need to capitalize it or put commas around it, if it is not dialogue. (No one thought the idea of "going to the store" sounded very fun.)

Note that when the last word in a sentence has both a quotation mark and a period attached to it, the period is always inside the quotes. This is the case when you have a complete sentence inside a quote ("Let's go to the store."), and when the last word in a sentence just happens to have quote marks around it (Kerri said I was "mean.") You also need to do the same thing with commas. (Kerri said I was "mean," and it made me feel bad.) However, other punctuation marks such as colons, semicolons and dashes do not follow this rule and should come outside the quotes. (Kerri said I was "mean"; it made me feel bad.)

When you want to use a quote inside a quote, you use the standard double-quotation marks for the outer quote and single-quotation marks for the inner quote. ("The sign on the door said 'no soliciting,' so we went to the next house.")

Quotation marks are also used around certain types of titles. To figure out which ones, it helps to look at which titles are not put in quotes as well.

Titles are generally in two categories: large works and small works. Large works are things such as newspapers, magazines, CDs, books and television shows. The defining characteristic of a large work is that it is able to hold small works in it. Small works are the articles inside newspapers and magazines, the songs on a CD, the chapters in a book and the episodes of a television show. It is small works that get quotation marks around them. (Large works, meanwhile, are either underlined or italicized.)

Using quotation marks correctly in a title looks something like this: The two-page article entitled "San Francisco Giants Win World Series" appeared in yesterday's New York Times. The article title is in quotes, and the newspaper title is in italics.

Common English Usage Mistakes - A Quick Review

Like some parts of English grammar, usage is definitely going to be on the exam and there isn't any tricky strategies or shortcuts to help you get through this section.

Here is a quick review of common usage mistakes.

1. May and Might

'May' can act as a principal verb, which can express permission or possibility.

Examples:

Lets wait, the meeting may have started.
May I begin now?

'May' can act as an auxiliary verb, which an expresses a purpose or wish

Examples:

May you find favour in the sight of your employer.
May your wishes come true.
People go to school so that they may be educated.

The past tense of may is might.
Examples:

I asked if I might begin

'Might' can be used to signify a weak or slim possibility or polite suggestion.

Examples:

You might find him in his office, but I doubt it.
You might offer to help if you want to.

2. Lie and Lay

The verb lay should always take an object. The three forms of the verb lay are: laid, lay and laid.

The verb lie (recline) should not take any object. The three forms of the verb lie are: lay, lie and lain.

Examples:

Lay on the bed.
The tables were laid by the students.
Let the little kid lie.
The patient lay on the table.

The dog has lain there for 30 minutes.

Note: The verb lie can also mean "to tell a falsehood." This verb can appear in three forms: lied, lie, and lied. This is different from the verb lie (recline) mentioned above.

Examples:

The accused is fond of telling lies.
Did she lie?

3. Would and should

The past tense of shall is 'should', and so "should" generally follows the same principles as "shall."

The past tense of will is "would," and so "would" generally follows the same principles as "will."

The two verbs 'would and should' can be correctly used interchangeably to signify obligation. The two verbs also have some unique uses too. Should is used in three persons to signify obligation.

Examples:

I should go after work.
People should do exercises everyday.
You should be generous.

"Would" is specially used in any of the three persons, to signify willingness, determination and habitual action.

Examples:

They would go for a test run every Saturday.
They would not ignore their duties.
She would try to be punctual.

4. Principle and Auxiliary Verbs

Two principal verbs can be used along with one auxiliary verb when the auxiliary verb form suits the two principal verbs.

Examples:

A number of people have been employed and some promoted.

A new tree has been planted and the old has been cut down.

Again note the difference in the verb form.

5. Can and Could

A. Can is used to express capacity or ability.

Examples:

I can complete the assignment today
He can meet up with his target.

B. Can is also used to express permission.

Examples:

Yes, you can begin

In the sentence below, "can" was used to mean the same thing as "may." However, the difference is that the word "can" is used for negative or interrogative sentences, while "may" is used in affirmative sentences to express possibility.

Examples:

They may be correct.   Positive sentence - use may.
Can this statement be correct? A question using "can."
It cannot be correct. Negative sentence using "can."

The past tense of can is could. It can serve as a principal verb when it is used to express its own meaning.

Examples:

Despite the difficulty of the test, he could still perform well. "Could" here is used to express ability.

6. Ought

The verb ought should normally be followed by the word to.

Examples:

I *ought to* close shop now.

The verb 'ought' can be used to express:

A. Desirability

You ought to wash your hands before eating. It is desirable to wash your hands.

B. Probability

She ought to be on her way back by now. She is probably on her way.

C. Moral obligation or duty

The government ought to protect the oppressed. It is the government's duty to protect the oppressed.

7. Raise and Rise

Rise

The verb rise means to go up, or to ascend.
The verb rise can appear in three forms, rose, rise, and risen. The verb should not take an object.

Examples:

The bird rose very slowly.
The trees rise above the house.

My aunt has risen in her career.

Raise
The verb raise means to increase, to lift up.
The verb raise can appear in three forms, raised, raise and raised.

Examples:

He raised his hand.
The workers requested a raise.

Do not raise that subject.

8. Past Tense and Past Participle

Pay attention to the proper use these verbs: sing, show, ring, awake, fly, flow, begin, hang and sink.
Mistakes usually occur when using the past participle and past tense of these verbs as they are often mixed up.

Each of these verbs can appear in three forms:

Sing, Sang, Sung.
Show, Showed, Showed/Shown.
Ring, Rang, Rung.
Awake, awoke, awaken
Fly, Flew, Flown.
Flow, Flowed, Flowed.
Begin, Began, Begun.
Hang, Hanged, Hanged (a criminal)
Hang, Hung, Hung (a picture)
Sink, Sank, Sunk.

Examples:

The stranger rang the door bell. (simple past tense)
I have rung the door bell already. (past participle - an action completed in the past)

The stone sank in the river. (simple past tense)
The stone had already sunk. (past participle - an action completed in the past)

The meeting began at 4:00.

The meeting has begun.

9. Shall and Will

When speaking informally, the two can be used interchangeably. In formal writing, they must be used correctly.

"Will" is used in the second or third person, while "shall" is used in the first person. Both verbs are used to express a time or even in the future.

Examples:

I shall, We shall (First Person)
You will (Second Person)
They will (Third Person)

This principle however reverses when the verbs are to be used to express threats, determination, command, willingness, promise or compulsion. In these instances, will is now used in first person and shall in the second and third person.

Examples:

I will be there next week, no matter what.
This is a promise, so the first person "I" takes "will."

You shall ensure that the work is completed.
This is a command, so the second person "you" takes "shall."

I will try to make payments as promised.
This is a promise, so the first person "I" takes "will."

They shall have arrived by the end of the day.
This is a determination, so the third person "they" takes shall.

Note

A. The two verbs, shall and will, should not occur twice in the same sentence when the same future is being referred to

Example:

I shall arrive early if my driver is here on time.

B. Will should not be used in the first person when questions are being asked

Examples:

Shall I go?
Shall we go?

SUBJECT VERB AGREEMENT

Verbs in any sentence must agree with the subject of the sentence both in person and number. Problems usually occur when the verb doesn't correspond with the right subject or the verb fails to match the noun close to it.

Unfortunately, there is no easy way around these principals - no tricky strategy or easy rule. You just have to memorize them.

Here is a quick review:

The verb to be, present (past)

Person	Singular	Plural
First	I am (was)	we are (were)
Second	you are (were)	you are (were)
Third	he, she, it is (was)	they are (were)

The verb to have, present (past)

Person	Singular	Plural
First	I have (had)	we have (had)
Second	you have (had)	you have (had)
Third	he, she, it has (had)	they have (had)

Regular verbs, e.g. to walk, present (past)

Person	Singular	Plural
First	I walk (walked)	we walk (walked)
Second	you walk (walked)	you walk (walked)
Third	he, she, it walks (walked)	they work (walked)

1. Every and Each

When nouns are qualified by "every" or "each," they take a singular verb even if they are joined by 'and'

Examples:

Each mother and daughter was a given separate test.
Every teacher and student was properly welcomed.

2. Plural Nouns

Nouns like measles, tongs, trousers, riches, scissors etc. are all plural.
Examples:

The trousers are dirty.
My scissors have gone missing.
The tongs are on the table.

3. With and As Well

Two subjects linked by "with" or "as well" should have a verb that matches the first subject.

Examples:

The pencil, with the papers and equipment, is on the desk.
David as well as Louis is coming.

4. Plural Nouns

The following nouns take a singular verb:

politics, mathematics, innings, news, advice, summons, furniture, information, poetry, machinery, vacation, scenery

Examples:

The machinery is difficult to assemble
The furniture has been delivered
The scenery was beautiful

5. Single Entities

A proper noun in plural form that refers to a single entity requires a singular verb. This is a complicated way of saying; some things appear to be plural, but are really singular, or some nouns refer to a collection of things but the collection is really singular.

Examples:

The United Nations Organization is the decision maker in the matter.

Here the "United Nations Organization" is really only one "thing" or noun, but is made up of many "nations."

The book, "The Seven Virgins" was not available in the library.
Here there is only one book, although the title of the book is plural.

6. Specific Amounts are always singular

A plural noun that refers to a specific amount or quantity that is considered as a whole (dozen, hundred, score etc) requires a singular verb.

Examples:

60 minutes is quite a long time.
Here "60 minutes" is considered a whole, and therefore one item (singular noun).
The first million is the most difficult.

7. Either, Neither and Each are always singular

The verb is always singular when used with: either, each, neither, everyone and many.

Examples:

Either of the boys is lying.
Each of the employees has been well compensated
Many a police officer has been found to be courageous
Every one of the teachers is responsible

8. Linking with Either, Or, and Neither match the second subject

Two subjects linked by "either," "or," "nor" or "neither" should have a verb that matches the second subject.

Examples:

Neither David nor Paul will be coming.
Either Mary or Tina is paying.
Note
If one subject linked by "either," "or," "nor" or "neither" is in plural form, then the verb should also be in plural, and the verb should be close to the plural subject.

Examples:
Neither the mother nor her kids have eaten.
Either Mary or her friends are paying.

9. Collective Nouns are Plural

Some collective nouns such as poultry, gentry, cattle, vermin etc. are considered plural and require a plural verb.

Examples:

The poultry are sick.
The cattle are well fed.

Note
Collective nouns involving people can work with both plural and singular verbs.
Examples:

Nigerians are known to be hard working
Europeans live in Africa

10. Nouns that are Singular and Plural

Nouns like deer, sheep, swine, salmon etc. can be singular or plural and require the same verb form.

Examples:

The swine is feeding. (singular)
The swine are feeding. (plural)

The salmon is on the table. (singular)
The salmon are running upstream. (plural)

11. Collective Nouns are Singular

Collective nouns such as Army, Jury, Assembly, Committee, Team etc should carry a singular verb when they subscribe to one idea. If the ideas or views are more than one, then the verb should be plural.

Examples:

The committee is in agreement in their decision.

The committee were in disagreement in their decision.
The jury has agreed on a verdict.
The jury were unable to agree on a verdict.

12. Subjects links by "and" are plural.

Two subjects linked by "and" always require a plural verb

Examples:

David and John are students.

Note
If the subjects linked by "and" are used as one phrase, or constitute one idea, then the verb must be singular

The color of his socks and shoe is black.
Here "socks and shoe" are two nouns, however the subject is "color" which is singular.

MATHEMATICS

This section contains a self-assessment and math tutorials. The tutorials are designed to familiarize general principles and the self-assessment contains general questions similar to the math questions likely to be on the exam, but are not intended to be identical to the exam questions. The tutorials are not designed to be a complete math course, and it is assumed that students have some familiarity with math. If you do not understand parts of the tutorial, or find the tutorial difficult, it is recommended that you seek out additional instruction.

Tour of the BC Police Mathematics Content

Below is a detailed list of the mathematics topics likely to appear on the exam. Make sure that you understand these topics at the very minimum.

- Convert decimals, percent, roman numerals and fractions

- Solve word problems

- Calculate percent and ratio

- Operations using fractions, percent and fractions

- Analyze and interpret tables, graphs and charts

- Understand and solve simple algebra problems

- Simple Geometry

The questions in the self-assessment are not the same as you will find on the exam - that would be too easy! And nobody knows what the questions will be and they change all the time. Mostly, the changes consist of substituting new questions for old, but the changes also can be new question formats or styles, changes to the number of questions in each section, changes to the time limits for each section, and combining sections. So, while the format and exact wording of the questions may differ slightly, and changes from year to year, if you can answer the questions below, you will have no problem with the mathematics section.

MATHEMATICS SELF-ASSESSMENT

The purpose of the self-assessment is:

- Identify your strengths and weaknesses.

- Develop your personalized study plan (above)

- Get accustomed to the format

- Extra practice – the self-assessments are almost a full 3rd practice test!

- Provide a baseline score for preparing your study schedule.

Since this is a Self-assessment, and depending on how confident you are with Math, timing yourself is optional. This self-assessment has 15 questions, so allow about 15 minutes to complete.

Once complete, use the table below to assess your understanding of the content, and prepare your study schedule described in chapter 1.

80% - 100%	Excellent – you have mastered the content
60 – 79%	Good. You have a working knowledge. Even though you can just pass this section, you may want to review the tutorials and do some extra practice to see if you can improve your mark.
40% - 59%	Below Average. You do not understand the content. Review the tutorials, and retake this quiz again in a few days, before proceeding to the Practice Test Questions.
Less than 40%	Poor. You have a very limited understanding. Please review the tutorials, and retake this quiz again in a few days, before proceeding to the Practice Test Questions.

Math Self-Assessment

	A	B	C	D	E		A	B	C	D	E
1	○	○	○	○	○	21	○	○	○	○	○
2	○	○	○	○	○	22	○	○	○	○	○
3	○	○	○	○	○	23	○	○	○	○	○
4	○	○	○	○	○						
5	○	○	○	○	○						
6	○	○	○	○	○						
7	○	○	○	○	○						
8	○	○	○	○	○						
9	○	○	○	○	○						
10	○	○	○	○	○						
11	○	○	○	○	○						
12	○	○	○	○	○						
13	○	○	○	○	○						
14	○	○	○	○	○						
15	○	○	○	○	○						
16	○	○	○	○	○						
17	○	○	○	○	○						
18	○	○	○	○	○						
19	○	○	○	○	○						
20	○	○	○	○	○						

Math Self-Assessment

1. A motorcycle is traveling at 100 km/hr. How far will it travel in 2 minutes?

    a. 1.6
    b. 3.3
    c. 1
    d. 12.5

2. Bill invests $4,000 at 8% compounded yearly. How much will he have in 2 years?

    a. $4320.00
    b. $4665.60
    c. $4640.00
    d. $4800.00

3. A waitress serves 10 tables one evening on her shift from 6 - 12:00 PM. She makes $10.50 per hour plus tips. Her total bills come to $240.60 with an average tip of 12%. How much did she make?

    a. $28.87
    b. $63.00
    c. $91.87
    d. $81.87

4. 15 is what percent of 200?

    a. 7.5%
    b. 15%
    c. 20%
    d. 17.50%

5. A boy has 5 red balls, 3 white balls and 2 yellow balls. What percent of the balls are yellow?

    a. 2%
    b. 8%
    c. 20%
    d. 12%

6. Add 10% of 300 to 50% of 20

    a. 50%
    b. 40%
    c. 60%
    d. 45%

7. Convert 75% to a fraction.

    a. 2/100
    b. 75/100
    c. 3/4
    d. 4/7

8. Convert 90% to a fraction

    a. 1/10
    b. 9/9
    c. 10/100
    d. 9/10

9. A man buys an item for $420 and has a balance of $3000.00. How much did he have before?

    a. $2,580
    b. $3,420
    c. $2,420
    d. $342

10. Divide 9.60 by 3.2

    a. 2.50
    b. 3
    c. 2.3
    d. 6.4

11. If X = 7 solve 3x + 5 − 2x

    a. x = 6
    b. x = 12
    c. x = 1
    d. x = 0

12. Solve $\sqrt{121}$

    a. 11
    b. 23
    c. 12
    d. 9

13. Solve 3x − 27 = 0

    a. x = 24
    b. x = 30
    c. x = 9
    d. x = 21

14. Solve the following equation 4(y + 6) = 3y + 30

    a. y = 6
    b. y = 20
    c. y = 30/7
    d. y = 30

15. Solve √144

    a. 14
    b. 72
    c. 24
    d. 12

16. √75 + √48 - √(3 / 0.01) =

    a. - √3
    b. √3
    c. 3
    d. 3√3

17. x = a + bi and y = a - bi. If x * y = 5a², find one possible value of b in terms of a.

    a. a
    b. 2a
    c. 3a
    d. 4a

18. Factor the polynomial $x^3y^3 - x^2y^8$.

    a. $x^2y^3(x - y^5)$
    b. $x^3y^3(1 - y^5)$
    c. $x^2y^2(x - y^6)$
    d. $xy^3(x - y^5)$

19. We are given that A = (√3 - 1) / (√5 + 1) and B = (√5 - 1) / (√3 + 1). What is the value of A in terms of B?

    a. B/2
    b. 3B/2
    c. 2B
    d. 3B

20. Using the factoring method, solve the quadratic equation: $x^2 - 5x - 6 = 0$

    a. -6 and 1
    b. -1 and 6
    c. 1 and 6
    d. -6 and -1

21. Find 2 numbers that sum to 21 and the sum of the squares is 261.

    a. 14 and 7
    b. 15 and 6
    c. 16 and 5
    d. 17 and 4

22. Using the factoring method, solve the quadratic equation: $x^2 + 4x + 4 = 0$

    a. 0 and 1
    b. 1 and 2
    c. 2
    d. -2

23. $(3y^5 - 2y + y^4 + 2y^3 + 5) + (2y^5 + 3y^3 + 2 + 7y)$

    a. $5y^5 + y^4 + 5y^3 + 5y + 7$
    b. $5y^3 + y^4 + 5y^3$
    c. $5y^5 + y^3 + 7y^3 + 5y + 5$
    d. $5y^2 + y^4 + 5y^3 + 7y + 5$

Answer Key

1. B
First calculate the distance traveled in 1 minute.
100 km/hr. = 100/60 = 1.666 km/minute.
So, in 2 minutes the motorcycle will travel 3.33 kilometers.

2. B
For the first year, $4,000 invested at 8% will be 4000 X .08 = 320. The interest is compounded yearly, so to calculate the second years interest, 4320 X .08 = 345.60.
The total will then be 4320 + 345.60 = $4665.60

3. C
First calculate her hourly wage. 6 hours X 10.50/hour = $63. Next calculate tips. $240.60 X .12 = $28.87. So her total earnings will be 63 + 28.87 = 91.87

4. A
15% = 15/100 X 200 = 7.5%

5. C
Total no. of balls = 10, no. of yellow balls = 2. 2/10 X 100 = 20%

6. B
10% of 300 = 30 and 50% of 20 = 10 so 30 + 10 = 40.

7. C
75% = 75/100 = 3/4

8. D
90% = 90/100 = 9/10

9. B
(Amount Spent) $420 + $3000 (Balance) = $3,420

10. B
9.60/3.2 = 3

11. B
X = 7, so 3x = 3 x 7 = 21, 2x = 2 x 7 = 14, so 21 + 5 - 14 = 26 - 14 = 12

12. A
$\sqrt{121}$ = 11

13. C
3x = 27, x = 27/3, x = 9

14. A
4y + 24 = 3y + 30, = 4y – 3y + 24 = 30, = y + 24 = 30, = y = 30 – 24, = y = 6

15. D
$\sqrt{144}$ = 12.

16. A
Here, we see that the numbers inside the roots are not prime numbers, so we may find perfect square multipliers inside these numbers. Then, we can take these numbers out of the root as factors:

$\sqrt{75} + \sqrt{48} - \sqrt{(3 / 0.01)} = \sqrt{(3.25)} + \sqrt{(3.16)} - \sqrt{(3 / 0.01)}$

$= \sqrt{(3.5^2)} + \sqrt{(3.4^2)} - \sqrt{(3 / 0.1^2)}$

$= 5\sqrt{3} + 4\sqrt{3} - (1/0.1)\sqrt{3}$

Here, notice that 1/0.1 = 10/1 = 10:

$= (5 + 4 - 10)\sqrt{3}$

$= - \sqrt{3}$

17. B

In this type of questions, it is essential to recall that $i^2 = -1$.

We are given that $x = a + bi$ and $y = a - bi$. To find $x * y$, we need to multiply these two expressions:

$x * y = (a + bi)(a - bi) = a^2 - abi + abi - b^2i^2 = a^2 + b^2$
So, $x.y = a^2 + b^2 = 5a^2$
Then, $b^2 = 4a^2$

To obtain b alone, take the square root of both sides:
$\sqrt{b^2} = \sqrt{4a^2}$

$b = 2a$ and $b = -2a$
There are two possible solutions for b: 2a and -2a. We only find 2a in the answer choices.

18. A

We need to find the greatest common divisor of the two terms to factor the expression. We should remember that if the bases of the exponents is the same, the product is found by summing the powers and writing on the same base. Similarly; when dividing, the power of the divisor is subtracted from the power of the divided.

Both x^3y^3 and x^2y^8 contain x^2 and y^3. So,

$x^3y^3 - x^2y^8 = x * x^2y^3 - y^5 * x^2y^3$ ... We can take x^2y^3 out as the factor:

$= x^2y^3(x - y^5)$

19. A

Notice that the denominator of A and numerator of B; numerator of A and denominator of B are conjugates. If we equate the denominators of both A and B at the same number; it is easier to write A in terms of B.

$A = (\sqrt{3} - 1) / (\sqrt{5} + 1)$ $_{(\sqrt{3} + 1)}$

$= ((\sqrt{3} - 1) * (\sqrt{3} + 1)) / ((\sqrt{5} + 1) * (\sqrt{3} + 1)) = (3 - 1) / ((\sqrt{5} + 1) * (\sqrt{3} + 1))$

$= 2 / ((\sqrt{5} + 1) * (\sqrt{3} + 1))$

B = (√5 - 1) / (√3 + 1) $_{(√5 + 1)}$

= ((√5 - 1) * (√5 + 1)) / ((√5 + 1) * (√3 + 1))

= (5 - 1) / ((√5 + 1) * (√3 + 1))

= 4 / ((√5 + 1) * (√3 + 1))

There is no need to expand the denominators of the new forms of A and B since they are the same. Comparing the numerators is sufficient. Notice that B is 2 times A. So, A = B/2.

20. B
Solve $x^2 - 5x - 6 = 0$ using the factoring method.

We try to separate the middle term -5x to find common factors with x^2 and -6 separately:

$x^2 - 6x + x - 6 = 0$ ... Here, we see that x is a common factor for x^2 and -6x:

x(x - 6) + x - 6 = 0 ... Here, we have x times x - 6 and 1 time x - 6 summed up. This means that we have x + 1 times x - 6:

(x + 1)(x - 6) = 0 ... This is true when either or both of the expressions in the parenthesis are equal to zero:

x + 1 = 0 ... x = -1

x - 6 = 0 ... x = 6

-1 and 6 are the solutions for this quadratic equation.

21. B
There are two statements made. This means that we can write two equations according to these statements:
The sum of two numbers are 21: x + y = 21

The sum of the squares is 261: $x^2 + y^2 = 261$

We are asked to find x and y.

Since we have the sums of the numbers and the sums of their squares; we can use the square formula of x + y, that is:

$(x + y)^2 = x^2 + 2xy + y^2$ ... Here, we can insert the known values $x + y$ and $x^2 + y^2$:

$(21)^2 = 261 + 2xy$ ... Arranging to find xy:

$441 = 261 + 2xy$

$441 - 261 = 2xy$

$180 = 2xy$

$xy = 180/2$

$xy = 90$

We need to find two numbers which multiply to 90. Checking the answer choices, we see that in (b), 15 and 6 are given. 15 * 6 = 90. Also their squares sum up to 261 ($15^2 + 6^2 = 225 + 36 = 261$). So these two numbers satisfy the equation.

22. D
$x^2 + 4x + 4 = 0$ ... We try to separate the middle term 4x to find common factors with x^2 and 4 separately:

$x^2 + 2x + 2x + 4 = 0$ ... Here, we see that x is a common factor for x^2 and 2x, and 2 is a common factor for 2x and 4:

$x(x + 2) + 2(x + 2) = 0$ ... Here, we have x times $x + 2$ and 2 times $x + 2$ summed up. This means that we have $x + 2$ times $x + 2$:

$(x + 2)(x + 2) = 0$

$(x + 2)^2 = 0$ ... This is true if only if $x + 2$ is equal to zero.

$x + 2 = 0$

$x = -2$

23. A
Write in standard form $(3y^5 + y^4 + 2y^3 - 2y + 5) + (2y^5 + 3y^3 + 7y + 2)$

Arrange in columns of like terms and then add

$3y^5 + y^4 + 2y^3 - 2y + 5$
$2y^5 + 3y^3 + 7y + 2$

$5y^5 + y^4 + 5y^3 + 5y + 7$

Basic Math Video Tutorials

https://www.test-preparation.ca/math-videos/

Fraction Tips, Tricks and Shortcuts

When you are writing an exam, time is precious, so anything you can do to answer questions faster is a real advantage.

Here are some ideas, shortcuts, tips and tricks that can speed up answering fraction problems.

Remember that a fraction is just a number which names a portion of something. For instance, instead of having a whole pie, a fraction says you have a part of a pie--such as a half of one or a fourth of one.

Two numbers make up a fraction. The number on top is the numerator. The number on the bottom is the denominator.

To remember which is which, just remember that "denominator" and "down" both start with a "d." And the "downstairs" number is the denominator. So for instance, in ½, the numerator is 1, and the denominator (or "downstairs") number is 2.

Adding Fractions

It's easy to add two fractions if they have the same denominator. Just add the digits on top and leave the bottom one the same: 1/10 + 6/10 = 7/10.

It's the same with subtracting fractions with the same denominator: 7/10 - 6/10 = 1/10.

Adding and subtracting fractions with different denominators is more complicated.

First, you have to arrange the fractions so they have the same denominators.

The easiest way to do this is to multiply the denominators: For 2/5 + 1/2 multiply 5 by 2. Now you have a denominator of 10.

But now you have to change the top numbers too. Since you multiplied the 5 in 2/5 by 2, you also multiply the 2 by 2, to get 4. So the first fraction is now 4/10.

In the second fraction, you multiplied the denominator by 5, you have to multiply the numerator by 5 also, to get 5/10.

Now you have 4/10 + 5/10 and you can add 5 and 4 to get 9/10.

Simplest Form

To reduce a fraction to its simplest form, you have to arrange the numerator and denominator so the only common factor is 1.

Think of it this way:

Let's take an example: The fraction 2/10.

This is not reduced to its simplest terms because there is a number that will divide evenly into both: 2. We want to make it so that the only number that will divide evenly into both is 1.

Divide the top and bottom by 2 to get the new, reduced fraction - 1/5.

Multiplying Fractions

This is the easiest of all: Just multiply the two top numbers and then multiply the two bottom numbers.

Here is an example,

2/5 X 2/3

First, multiply the numerators: 2 X 2 = 4

then multiply the denominators: 5 X 3 = 15

Your answer is 4/15.

Dividing Fractions

Dividing fractions is easy if you remember a simple trick - first turn the second fraction upside down - then multiply!

Here is an example:

7/8 X 1/2

Turn the second fraction upside down:

7/8 X 2/1

then multiply:

(7 X 2) / (8 X 1) = 14/8

CONVERTING FRACTIONS TO DECIMALS

There are a couple of ways to convert fractions to decimals. The first, which is the fastest -- is to memorize some basic fraction facts.

1/100 is "one hundredth," expressed as a decimal, it's .01.

> 1/50 is "two hundredths," expressed as a decimal, it's .02.

> 1/25 is "one twenty-fifth" or "four hundredths," expressed as a decimal, it's .04.

1/20 is "one twentieth" or ""five hundredths," expressed as a decimal, it's .05.

1/10 is "one tenth," expressed as a decimal, it's .1.

1/8 is "one eighth," or "one hundred twenty-five thousandths," expressed as a decimal, it's .125.

1/5 is "one fifth," or "two tenths," expressed as a decimal, it's .2.

1/4 is "one fourth" or "twenty-five hundredths," expressed as a decimal, it's .25.

1/3 is "one third" or "thirty-three hundredths," expressed as a decimal, it's .33.

1/2 is "one half" or "five tenths," expressed as a decimal, it's .5.

3/4 is "three fourths," or "seventy-five hundredths," expressed as a decimal, it's .75.

Of course, if you're no good at memorization, another good technique for converting a fraction to a decimal is to manipulate it so that the fraction's denominator is 10, 100, 1000, or some other power of 10.

Here's an example: We'll start with three quarters. What is the first number in the 4 "times table" that you can multiply and get a multiple of 10? Can you multiply 4 by something to get 10? No. Can you multiply it by something to get 100? Yes! 4 X 25 is 100.

So multiply the numerator by 25, which is 75 over 100

We know fractions are really a division problem, and we also know that dividing by 100, means we move the decimal 2 places to the left.

So, 75 over 100 = .75

Lets try another example - Convert one fifth to a decimal.

First find a power of 10 that 5 goes into evenly, which is 2.

Multiply the numerator and denominator by 2, which is two tenths.

Dividing 2 by 10 means we move the decimal place 1 place to the left.

So one fifth = zero point two

Converting Fractions to Percent

Here is a quick method to convert fraction to percent and a strategy for answering on a multiple choice test that will save you valuable exam time.

First, remember that a fraction is a division problem: you're dividing the bottom number into the top.

Taking an example, convert 2/3 into percent.

The first method is to multiple the numerator by 100 and divide. So,

(2 X 100) / 2 = 100/3 = 66.66

Add a % sign and you have the answer, 66.66%

If you're doing these conversions on a multiple-choice test, here's an idea that might be even easier and faster. Let's say you have a fraction of 1/8 and you're asked to convert to percent.

Since we know that "percent" means hundredths, ask yourself what number we can multiply 8 by to get 100. Since there is no number, ask what number gets us close to 100.

That number is 12: 8 X 12 = 96. So it gets us a little less than 100. Now, whatever you do to the denominator, you have to do to the numerator. Let's multiply 1 X 12 and we get 12. However, since 96 is a little less than 100, we know that our answer will be a little MORE than 12%.

Look at the choices and eliminate the obvious wrong choices. So if your possible answers on the multiple-choice test are these:

a) 8.5% b) 19% c) 12.5% d) 25%

then we know the answer is c) 12.5%, because it's a little MORE than the 12 we got in our math problem above.

Here all the choices except choice C 12.5% can be eliminated.

You don't have to know the exact correct answer, just enough to estimate, then eliminate the obviously wrong answers.

This was an easy example to demonstrate the strategy, but don't be fooled! You probably won't get such an easy question on your exam. By estimating your answer quickly, then eliminating obviously incorrect choices immediately, you save precious exam time.

CONVERTING DECIMALS TO FRACTIONS

Converting decimals to fractions is easy if you say it the right way! If you say "point one" or "point 25," you'll have trouble.

But if you say, "one tenth" and "twenty-five hundredths," then you have already solved it! That's because, if you know your fractions, you know that "one tenth" looks like this: 1/10. And "twenty-five hundredths" looks like this: 25/100.

Even if you have digits before the decimal, such as 3.4, learning how to say the word will help you with the conversion into a fraction. It's not "three point four," it's "three and four tenths." Knowing this, you know that the fraction which looks like "three and four tenths" is 3 4/10.

The conversion is not complete until you reduce the fraction to its lowest terms: It's not 25/100, but 1/4.

Converting Decimals to Percent

Changing a decimal to a percent is easy if you remember one thing: multiply by 100.

For example, if you start with .45, simply multiply it by 100 for 45. Then add the % sign to the end - 45%.

Think of it this way: take out the decimal point, add a percent sign on the opposite side. In other words, the decimal on the left is replaced by the % on the right.

It doesn't work quite that easily if the decimal is in the middle of the number. For example, 3.7. Here, take out the decimal in the middle and replace it with a 0 % at the end. So 3.7 converted to decimal is 370%.

Solving One-Variable Linear Equations

Linear equations with variable x is an equation with the following form:
$$ax = b$$

where a and b are real numbers. If a=0 and b is different from 0, then the equation has no solution.

Let's solve one simple example of a linear equation with one variable:
$$4x - 2 = 2x + 6$$

When we are given this type of equation, we are always moving variables to the one side, and real numbers to the other side of the equals sign. Always remember: if you are changing sides, you are changing signs. Let's move all variables to the left, and real number to the right side:

$4x - 2 = 2x + 6$
$4x - 2x = 6 + 2$
$2x = 8$
$x = 8:2$
$x = 4$

When 2x goes to the left it becomes -2x, and -2 goes to the right and becomes +2. After calculations, we find that x is 4, which is a solution of our linear equation.

Let's solve a little more complex linear equation:

$2x - 6/4 + 4 = x$
$2x - 6 + 16 = 4x$
$2x - 4x = -16 + 6$
$-2x = -10$
$x = -10/-2$
$x = 5$

We multiply whole equation by 4, to lose the fractional line. Now we have a simple linear equation. If we change sides, we change the signs.

Solving Two-Variable Linear Equations

If we have 2 or more linear equations with 2 or more variables, then we have a system of linear equations. The idea here is to express one variable using the other in one equation, and then use it in the second equation, so we get a linear equation with one variable. Here is an example:

$x - y = 3$
$2x + y = 9$

From the first equation, we express y using x.

$y = x - 3$

In the second equation, we write x-3 instead of y. And there we get a linear equation with one variable x.

2x + x - 3 = 9
3x = 9 + 3
3x = 12
x = 12/3
x = 4

Now that we found x, we can use it to find y.

y = x - 3
y = 4 - 3
y = 1

So, the solution of this system is (x,y) = (4,1).

Let's solve one more system using a different method:

Solve:

5x - 3y = 17
x + 3y = 11

5x - 3y + x + 3y = 17 - 11

Notice that we have -3y in the first equation and +3y in the second. If we add these 2, we get zero, which means we lose variable y. So, we add these 2 equations and we get a linear equation with one variable.

6x = 6
x = 1

Now that we have x, we use it to find y.

5 - 3y = 17
-3y = 17 - 5
-3y = 12
y = 12/(-3)
y = -4

Adding and Subtracting Polynomials

When we are adding or subtracting 2 or more polynomials, we have to first group the same variables (arguments) that have the same degrees and then add or subtract them. For example, if we have ax^3 in one polynomial (where a is some real number), we have to group it with bx^3 from the other polynomial (where b is also some real number). Here is one example with adding polynomials:

$(-x^2 + 2x + 3) + (2x^2 + 4x - 5) =$
$-x^2 + 2x + 3 + 2x^2 + 4x - 5 =$
$x^2 + 6x - 2$

We remove the brackets, and since we have a plus in front of every bracket, the signs in the polynomials don't change. We group variables with the same degrees. We have -1 + 2, which is 1 and that's how we got x^2. For the first degree, where we have 2 + 4 which is 6, and the constants (real numbers) where we have 3 - 5 which is -2.

The principle is the same with subtracting, only we have to keep in mind that a minus in front of the polynomial changes all signs in that polynomial. Here is one example:

$(4x^3 - x^2 + 3) - (-3x^2 - 10) =$
$4x^3 - x^2 + 3 + 3x^2 + 10 =$
$4x^3 + 2x^2 + 13$

We remove the brackets, and since we have a minus in front of the second polynomial, all signs in that polynomial change. We have -3 x 2 and with minus in front, it becomes a plus and same goes for -10.

Now we group the variables with same degrees: there is no variable with the third degree in the second polynomial, so we just write 4 x 3. We group other variables the same way as adding polynomials.

Multiplying and Dividing Polynomials

If we have two polynomials that we need to multiply, then multiply each member of the first polynomial with each member of the second. Let's see in one example how this works:

$(x-1)(x-2) = x^2 - 2x - x + 2 = x^2 - 3x + 2$

The first member of the first polynomial is multiplied with the first member of the second polynomial and then with the second member of the second polynomial. Continue the process with the second member of the first polynomial, then simplify.

To multiply more polynomials, multiply the first 2, then multiply that result with next polynomial and so on. Here is one example:

$(1 - x)(2 - x)(3 - x) = (2 - x - 2x + x^2)(3-x)$
$= (2 - 3x + x^2)(3 - x)$
$= 6 - 2x - 9x + 3x^2 + 3x^2 - x^3 = 6 - 11x + 6x^2 - x^3$

Simplifying Polynomials

Let's say we are given some expression with one or more variables, where we have to add, subtract and multiply polynomials. We do the calculations with variables and constants and then we group the variables with the appropriate degrees. As a result, we get a polynomial. This process is called simplifying polynomials, where we go from a complex expression to a simple polynomial.

Example:

Simplify the following expression and arrange the degrees from bigger to smaller:

$4 + 3x - 2x^2 + 5x + 6x^3 - 2x^2 + 1 = 6x^3 - 4x^2 + 8x + 5$

We can have more complex expressions such as:

$(x + 5)(1 - x) - (2x - 2) = x - x^2 + 5 - 5x - 2x + 2 = -x^2 - 6x + 7$

Here, first we multiply the polynomials and then we subtract the result and the third polynomial.

Factoring Polynomials

If we have a polynomial that we want to write as multiplication of a real number and a polynomial or as a multiplication of 2 or more polynomials, then we are dealing with factoring polynomials.

Let's see an example for a simple factoring:

$12x^2 + 6x - 4 =$
$2 * 6x^2 + 2 * 3x - 2 * 2 =$
$2(6x^2 + 3x - 2)$

We look at every polynomial member as a product of a real number and a variable. Notice that all real numbers in the polynomial are even, so they have the same number (factor). We pull out that 2 in front of the polynomial, and we write what is left.

What if have a more complex case, where we can't find a factor that is a real number? Here is an example:

$x^2 - 2x + 1 =$
$x^2 - x - x + 1 =$
$x(x - 1) - (x - 1) =$
$(x - 1)(x - 1)$

We can write -2x as –x-x . Now we group first 2 members and we see that they have the same factor x, which we can pull in front of them. For the other 2 members, we pull the

minus in front of them, so we can get the same binomial that we got with the first 2 members. Now we have that this binomial is the factor for x(x-1) and (x-1).
If we pull x-1 in front (underlined), from the first member, we are left with x, and from the second we have -1.
And that is how we transform a polynomial into a product of 2 polynomials (here, binomials).

QUADRATIC EQUATIONS

A. Factoring

Quadratic equations are called second degree equations, which means that the second degree is the highest degree of the variable that can be found in the quadratic equation. The form of these equations is:

$ax^2 + bx + c = 0$

where a, b and c are some real numbers.

One way for solving quadratic equations is the factoring method, where we transform the quadratic equation into a product of 2 or more polynomials. Let's see how that works in one simple example:

$x^2 + 2x = 0$

$x(x+2) = 0$

$(x = 0) \vee (x + 2 = 0)$

$(x = 0) \vee (x = -2)$

Notice that here we don't have parameter c, but this is still a quadratic equation, because we have the second degree of variable x. Our factor here is x, which we put in front, and we are left with x+2. The equation is equal to 0, so either x or x+2 are 0, or both are 0.
So, our 2 solutions are 0 and -2.

B. Quadratic formula

If we are unsure how to rewrite quadratic equations so we can solve it using the factoring method, we can use the formula for quadratic equation:

$$x_{1,2} = \frac{-b \pm \sqrt{b^2 - 4ac}}{2a}$$

We write $x_{1,2}$ because it represents 2 solutions of the equation. Here is one example:

$3x^2 - 10x + 3 = 0$

$x_{1,2} = \frac{-b \pm \sqrt{b^2 - 4ac}}{2a}$

$x_{1,2} = \frac{-(-10) \pm \sqrt{(-10)^2 - 4 \cdot 3 \cdot 3}}{2 \cdot 3}$

$x_{1,2} = \frac{10 \pm \sqrt{100 - 36}}{6}$

$x_{1,2} = \frac{10 \pm \sqrt{64}}{6}$

$x_{1,2} = \frac{10 \pm 8}{6}$

$x_1 = \frac{10 + 8}{6} = \frac{18}{6} = 3$

$x_2 = \frac{10 - 8}{6} = \frac{2}{6} = \frac{1}{3}$

We see that a is 3, b is -10 and c is 3.

We use these numbers in the equation and do some calculations.

Notice that we have + and -, so x_1 is for + and x_2 is for -, and that's how we get 2 solutions.

Percent Tips, Tricks and Shortcuts

Percent problems are not nearly as scary as they appear, if you remember this neat trick:

Draw a cross as in:

Portion	Percent
Whole	100

In the upper left, write PORTION. In the bottom left, write WHOLE. In the top right, write PERCENT and in the bottom right, write 100. Whatever your problem is, you will leave blank the unknown, and fill in the other four parts. For example, let's suppose your problem is: Find 10% of 50. Since we know the 10% part, we put 10 in the percent corner. Since the whole number in our problem is 50, we put that in the corner marked whole. You always put 100 underneath the percent, so we leave it as is, which leaves only the top left corner blank. This is where we'll put our answer. Now simply multiply the two corner numbers that are NOT 100. Here, it's 10 X 50. That gives us 500. Now divide this by the remaining corner, or 100, to get a final answer of 5. 5 is the number that goes in the upper-left corner, and is your final solution.

Another hint to remember: Percents are the same thing as hundredths in decimals. So .45 is the same as 45 hundredths or 45 percent.

Converting Percents to Decimals

Percents are just a type of decimal, so it should be no surprise that converting between the two is actually fairly simple. Here are a few tricks and shortcuts to keep in mind:

- Remember that percent literally means "per 100" or "for every 100." So when you speak of 30% you're saying 30 for every 100 or the fraction 30/100. In basic math, you learned that fractions that have 10 or 100 as the denominator can easily be turned to a decimal. 30/100 is thirty hundredths, or expressed as a decimal, .30.
- Another way to look at it: To convert a percent to a decimal, simply divide the number by 100. So for instance, if the percent is 47%, divide 47 by 100. The result will be .47. Get rid of the % mark and you're done.
- Remember that the easiest way of dividing by 100 is by moving your decimal two spots to the left.

Converting Percent to Fractions

Converting Percent to Fractions is easy. After all, a percent is just a type of fraction; it tells you what part of 100 that you're talking about. Here are some simple ideas for making the conversion from a percent to a fraction:

- If the percent is a whole number -- say 34% -- then simply write a fraction with 100 as the denominator (the bottom number). Then put the percentage itself on top. So 34% becomes 34/100.
- Now reduce as you would reduce any percent. Here, by dividing 2 into 34 and 2 into 100, you get 17/50.
- If your percent is not a whole number -- say 3.4% --then convert it to a decimal expressed as hundredths. 3.4 is the same as 3.40 (or 3 and forty hundredths). Now ask yourself how you would express "three and forty hundredths" as a fraction. It would, of course, be 3 40/100. Reduce this and it becomes 3 2/5.

Exponents: Tips, Shortcuts & Tricks

Exponents are just shorthand for saying that you're multiplying a number by itself two or more times.

For instance, instead of saying 5 x 5 x 5, you can show that you're multiplying 5 by itself 3 times if you just write 5^3.

We usually say this as "five to the third power" or "five to the power of three." In this example, the raised 3 is an "exponent," and the 5 is the "base."

You can even use exponents with fractions. For instance, $1/2^3$ means you're multiplying 1/2 x 1/2 x 1/2. (The answer is 1/8).

Multiplying Exponents

For exponents with the same base, for instance 5^3 X 5^2, add the exponents and keep the base. The answer, then, is 5^5.

If the bases are different, for example, in 5^3 X 3^2, you have to do the math the long way to figure it out.

5 x 5 x 5 = 125, and 3 X 3 = 9.

125 X 9 = 1125

Dividing Exponents

For exponents with the same base, subtract the exponents. In the problem above, 5^3 X 5^2, 3 - 2 = 1. 5 to the power of 1 is 5.

Here are some quick things to remember

Any number to the power of 1 is that number.

Any number raised to the power of 0 is 1.

Number (x)	X^2	X^3
1	1	1
2	4	8
3	9	27
4	16	64
5	25	125
6	36	216
7	49	343
8	64	512
9	81	729
10	100	1000

How to Answer Basic Math Multiple Choice

The time allowed on the math portion of a standardized test is typically so short that there's no room for error. You have to be fast and accurate.

Math strategy is very helpful, but nothing beats knowing your stuff! Make sure that you have learned all the important formulas that will be used.

If you don't know the formulas, strategy won't help you.

How to Answer Basic Math Questions - the Basics

First, read the problem, but not the answers.

Work through the problem first and come up with your own answers. Hopefully, you should find your answer among the choices.
If no answer matches the one you got, re-check your math, but this time, use a different method. In math, there are different ways to solve a problem.

Math Multiple Choice Strategy

The two strategies for working with basic math multiple choice are Estimation and Elimination.

Estimation is just as it sounds - try to estimate an approximate answer first. Then look at the choices.

Elimination is probably the most powerful strategy for answering multiple choice.

Eliminate obviously incorrect answers and narrowing the possible choices.

Here are a few basic math examples of how this works.

Solve 2/3 + 5/12

    a. 9/17
    b. 3/11
    c. 7/12
    d. 1 1/12

First estimate the answer. 2/3 is more than half and 5/12 is about half, so the answer is going to be very close to 1.

Next, Eliminate. Choice A is about 1/2 and can be eliminated, choice B is very small, less than 1/2 and can be eliminated. Choice C is close to 1/2 and can be eliminated. Leaving only choice D, which is just over 1.

Work through the solution, find a common denominator and add. The correct answer is 1 1/12, so Choice D is correct.

Let's look at another example:

Solve 4/5 – 2/3

    a. 2/2
    b. 2/13
    c. 1
    d. 2/15

First, quickly estimate the answer. 4/5 is very close to 1, and 2/3 more than half, so the answer is going to be less than 1/2.

Choice A can be eliminated right away, because it is 1. Choice C can be eliminated for the same reason.

Next, look at the denominators. Since 5 and 3 don't go into 13, choice B can be eliminated as well.

That leaves choice D. Checking the answer, the common denominator will be 15. So the answer is 2/15 and choice D is correct.

Fractions shortcut - Canceling out.

In any operation with fractions, if the numerator of one fraction has a common multiple with the denominator of the other, you can cancel out. This saves time, and simplifies the problem quickly, making it easier to manage.

Solve 2/15 ÷ 4/5

    a. 6/65

    b. 6/75

    c. 5/12

    d. 1/6

To divide fractions, we multiply the first fraction with the inverse of the second fraction. Therefore we have 2/15 x 5/4. The numerator of the first fraction, 2, shares a multiple with the denominator of the second fraction, 4, which is 2. These cancel out, which gives, 1/3 x 1/2 = 1/6

Canceling Out solved the questions very quickly, but we can still use multiple choice strategies to answer.

Choice B can be eliminated because 75 is too large a denominator. Choice C can be eliminated because 5 and 15 don't go into 12.

Choice D is correct.

Decimal Multiple Choice Strategy and Shortcuts.

Multiplying decimals gives a very quick way to estimate and eliminate choices. Anytime that you multiply decimals, it is going to give an answer with the same number of decimal places as the combined operands.

So for example,

2.38 X 1.2 will produce a number with three places of decimal, which is 2.856.

Here are a few examples with step-by-step explanation:

Solve 2.06 x 1.2

    a. 24.82

    b. 2.482

    c. 24.72

    d. 2.472

This is a simple question, but even before you start calculating, you can eliminate several choices. When multiplying decimals, there will always be as many numbers behind the decimal place in the answer as the sum of the ones in the initial problem, so choices A and C can be eliminated.

The correct answer is D: 2.06 x 1.2 = 2.472

Solve 20.0 ÷ 2.5

    a. 12.05

    b. 9.25

    c. 8.3

    d. 8

First estimate the answer to be around 10, and eliminate choice A. And since it'd also be an even number, you can eliminate Choices B and C, leaving only choice D.

The correct answer is D: 20.0 ÷ 2.5 = 8

TYPES OF WORD PROBLEMS

Word problems can be classified into 12 types. Below are examples of each type with a complete solution. Some types of word problems can be solved quickly using multiple choice strategies and some cannot. Always look for ways to estimate the answer and then eliminate choices.

1. Age

A girl is 10 years older than her brother. By next year, she will be twice the age of her brother. What are their ages now?

    a. 25, 15

    b. 19, 9

    c. 21, 11

    d. 29, 19

Solution: B

We will assume that the girl's age is "a" and her brother's is "b." This means that based on the information in the first sentence,
a = 10 + b
Next year, she will be twice her brother's age, which gives
a + 1 = 2(b + 1)

We need to solve for one unknown factor and then use the answer to solve for the other. To do this we substitute the value of "a" from the first equation into the second equation. This gives

10 + b + 1 = 2b + 2
11 + b = 2b + 2
11 − 2 = 2b − b
b = 9

9 = b this means that her brother is 9 years old. Solving for the girl's age in the first equation gives a = 10 + 9. a = 19 the girl is aged 19. So, the girl is aged 19 and the boy is 9

2. Distance or speed

Two boats travel down a river towards the same destination, starting at the same time. One boat is traveling at 52 km/hr, and the other boat at 43 km/hr. How far apart will they be after 40 minutes?

    a. 46.67 km

    b. 19.23 km

    c. 6 km

    d. 14.39 km

Solution: C

After 40 minutes, the first boat will have traveled = 52 km/hr x 40 minutes/60 minutes = 34.66 km
After 40 minutes, the second boat will have traveled = 43 km/hr x 40/60 minutes = 28.66 km
Difference between the two boats will be 34.66 km − 28.66 km = 6 km.

Multiple Choice Strategy

First estimate the answer. The first boat is traveling 9 km. faster than the second, for 40 minutes, which is 2/3 of an hour. 2/3 of 9 = 6, as a rough guess of the distance apart.

Choices A, B and D can be eliminated right away.

3. Ratio

A recipe states that 700 grams of flour must be mixed in 100 ml of water, and 0.90 grams of salt added. A cook however has just 325 grams of flour. How much water and salt should be used?

    a. 0.41 grams and 46.4 ml
    b. 0.45 grams and 49.3 ml
    c. 0.39 grams and 39.8 ml
    d. 0.25 grams and 40.1 ml

Solution: A

The Cookbook states 700 grams of flour, but the cook only has 325. The first step is to determine the percentage of flour he has 325/700 x 100 = 46.4%
That means that 46.4% of all other items must also be used.
46.4% of 100 = 46.4 ml of water
46.4% of 0.90 = 0.41 grams of salt.

Multiple Choice Strategy

The recipe calls for 700 grams of flour but the cook only has 325, which is just less than half, the quantity of water and salt are going to be about half.

Choices C and D can be eliminated right away. Choice B is very close so be careful. Looking closely at Choice B, it is exactly half, and since 325 is slightly less than half of 700, it can't be correct.

Choice A is correct.

4. Percent

An agent received $6,685 as his commission for selling a property. If his commission was 13% of the selling price, how much was the property?

    a. $68,825
    b. $121,850
    c. $49,025
    d. $51,423

Solution: D

Let's assume that the property price is x
That means from the information given, 13% of x = 6,685
Solve for x,
x = 6685 x 100/13 = $51,423

Multiple Choice Strategy

The commission, 13%, is just over 10%, which is easier to work with. Round up $6685 to $6700, and multiple by 10 for an approximate answer. 10 X 6700 = $67,000. You can do this in your head. Choice B is much too big and can be eliminated. Choice C is too small and can be eliminated. Choices A and D are left and good possibilities.

Do the calculations to make the final choice.

5. Sales & Profit

A store owner buys merchandise for $21,045. He transports them for $3,905 and pays his staff $1,450 to stock the merchandise on his shelves. If he does not incur further costs, how much does he need to sell the items to make $5,000 profit?

    a. $32,500
    b. $29,350
    c. $32,400
    d. $31,400

Solution: D

Total cost of the items is $21,045 + $3,905 + $1,450 = $26,400
Total cost is now $26,400 + $5000 profit = $31,400

Multiple Choice Strategy

Round off and add the numbers up in your head quickly.
21,000 + 4,000 + 1500 = 26500. Add in 5000 profit for a total of 31500.

Choice B is too small and can be eliminated. Choice C and Choice A are too large and can be eliminated.

6. Tax/Income

A woman earns $42,000 per month and pays 5% tax on her monthly income. If the Government increases her monthly taxes by $1,500, what is her income after tax?

   a. $38,400
   b. $36,050
   c. $40,500
   d. $39, 500

Solution: A

Initial tax on income was 5/100 x 42,000 = $2,100
$1,500 was added to the tax to give $2,100 + 1,500 = $3,600
Income after tax left is $42,000 - $3,600 = $38,400

7. Interest

A man invests $3000 in a 2-year term deposit that pays 3% interest per year. How much will he have at the end of the 2-year term?

   a. $5,200
   b. $3,020
   c. $3,182.7
   d. $3,000

Solution: C

This is a compound interest problem. The funds are invested for 2 years and interest is paid yearly, so in the second year, he will earn interest on the interest paid in the first year.
3% interest in the first year = 3/100 x 3,000 = $90
At end of first year, total amount = 3,000 + 90 = $3,090
Second year = 3/100 x 3,090 = 92.7.
At end of second year, total amount = $3090 + $92.7 = $3,182.7

8. Averaging

The average weight of 10 books is 54 grams. 2 more books were added and the average weight became 55.4. If one of the 2 new books added weighed 62.8 g, what is the weight of the other?

  a. 44.7 g

  b. 67.4 g

  c. 62 g

  d. 52 g

Solution: C

Total weight of 10 books with average 54 grams will be = 10 × 54 = 540 g
Total weight of 12 books with average 55.4 will be = 55.4 × 12 = 664.8 g
So total weight of the remaining 2 will be= 664.8 – 540 = 124.8 g
If one weighs 62.8, the weight of the other will be= 124.8 g – 62.8 g = 62 g

Multiple Choice Strategy

Averaging problems can be estimated by looking at which direction the average goes. If additional items are added and the average goes up, the new items much be greater than the average. If the average goes down after new items are added, the new items must be less than the average.
Here, the average is 54 grams and 2 books are added which

increases the average to 55.4, so the new books must weight more than 54 grams.

Choices A and D can be eliminated right away.

9. Probability

A bag contains 15 marbles of various colors. If 3 marbles are white, 5 are red and the rest are black, what is the probability of randomly picking out a black marble from the bag?

    a. 7/15
    b. 3/15
    c. 1/5
    d. 4/15

Solution: A

Total marbles = 15
Number of black marbles = 15 − (3 + 5) = 7
Probability of picking out a black marble = 7/15

10. Two Variables

A company paid a total of $2850 to book for 6 single rooms and 4 double rooms in a hotel for one night. Another company paid $3185 to book for 13 single rooms for one night in the same hotel. What is the cost for single and double rooms in that hotel?

    a. single= $250 and double = $345
    b. single= $254 and double = $350
    c. single = $245 and double = $305
    d. single = $245 and double = $345

Solution: D

We can determine the price of single rooms from the information given of the second company. 13 single rooms =

3185.
One single room = 3185 / 13 = 245
The first company paid for 6 single rooms at $245. 245 x 6 = $1470
Total amount paid for 4 double rooms by first company = $2850 - $1470 = $1380
Cost per double room = 1380 / 4 = $345

11. Geometry

The length of a rectangle is 5 in. more than its width. The perimeter of the rectangle is 26 in. What is the width and length of the rectangle?

    a. width = 6 inches, Length = 9 inches

    b. width = 4 inches, Length = 9 inches

    c. width =4 inches, Length = 5 inches

    d. width = 6 inches, Length = 11 inches

Solution: B

Formula for perimeter of a rectangle is 2(L + W)
p=26, so 2(L + W) = p
The length is 5 inches more than the width, so
2(w + 5) + 2w = 26
2w + 10 + 2w = 26
2w + 2w = 26 - 10
4w = 16

W = 16/4 = 4 inches

L is 5 inches more than w, so L = 5 + 4 = 9 inches.

12. Totals and Fractions

A basket contains 125 oranges, mangoes and apples. If 3/5 of the fruits in the basket are mangoes and only 2/5 of the mangoes are ripe, how many ripe mangoes are there in the basket?

    a. 30
    b. 68
    c. 55
    d. 47

Solution: A
Number of mangoes in the basket is 3/5 x 125 = 75
Number of ripe mangoes = 2/5 x 75 = 30

Practice Test Questions Set 1

THE QUESTIONS BELOW ARE NOT THE SAME AS YOU WILL FIND ON THE BC POLICE ENTRANCE TEST- THAT WOULD BE TOO EASY! And nobody knows what the questions will be and they change all the time. Below are general questions that cover the same subject areas as the BC Police Entrance Test. So, while the format and exact wording of the questions may differ slightly, and change from year to year, if you can answer the questions below, you will have no problem with the BC Police Entrance Test.

For the best results, take these practice test questions as if it were the real exam. Set aside time when you will not be disturbed, and a location that is quiet and free of distractions. Read the instructions carefully, read each question carefully, and answer to the best of your ability.

Use the bubble answer sheets provided. When you have completed the practice questions, check your answer against the Answer Key and read the explanation provided.

Do not attempt more than one set of practice test questions in one day. After completing the first practice test, wait two or three days before attempting the second set of questions.

Reading Comprehension

	A B C D E		A B C D E
1	○ ○ ○ ○ ○	21	○ ○ ○ ○ ○
2	○ ○ ○ ○ ○	22	○ ○ ○ ○ ○
3	○ ○ ○ ○ ○	23	○ ○ ○ ○ ○
4	○ ○ ○ ○ ○	24	○ ○ ○ ○ ○
5	○ ○ ○ ○ ○	25	○ ○ ○ ○ ○
6	○ ○ ○ ○ ○	26	○ ○ ○ ○ ○
7	○ ○ ○ ○ ○	27	○ ○ ○ ○ ○
8	○ ○ ○ ○ ○	28	○ ○ ○ ○ ○
9	○ ○ ○ ○ ○	29	○ ○ ○ ○ ○
10	○ ○ ○ ○ ○	30	○ ○ ○ ○ ○
11	○ ○ ○ ○ ○		
12	○ ○ ○ ○ ○		
13	○ ○ ○ ○ ○		
14	○ ○ ○ ○ ○		
15	○ ○ ○ ○ ○		
16	○ ○ ○ ○ ○		
17	○ ○ ○ ○ ○		
18	○ ○ ○ ○ ○		
19	○ ○ ○ ○ ○		
20	○ ○ ○ ○ ○		

MEMORY

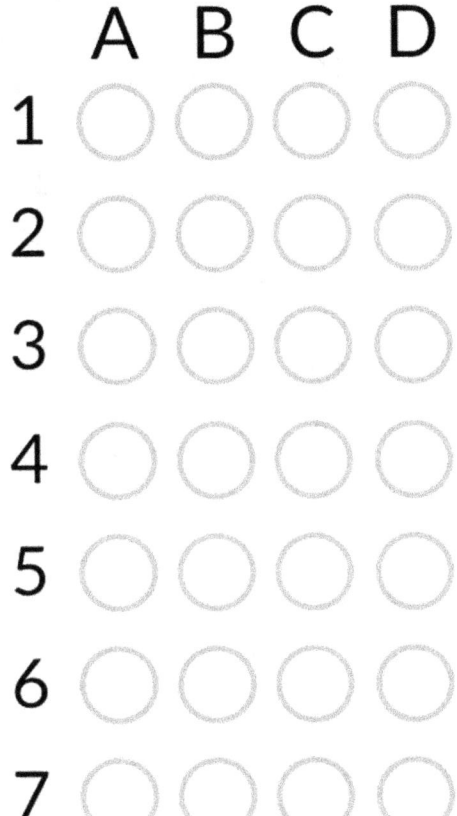

English

	A	B	C	D	E		A	B	C	D	E
1	○	○	○	○	○	21	○	○	○	○	○
2	○	○	○	○	○	22	○	○	○	○	○
3	○	○	○	○	○	23	○	○	○	○	○
4	○	○	○	○	○	24	○	○	○	○	○
5	○	○	○	○	○	25	○	○	○	○	○
6	○	○	○	○	○	26	○	○	○	○	○
7	○	○	○	○	○	27	○	○	○	○	○
8	○	○	○	○	○	28	○	○	○	○	○
9	○	○	○	○	○	29	○	○	○	○	○
10	○	○	○	○	○	30	○	○	○	○	○
11	○	○	○	○	○						
12	○	○	○	○	○						
13	○	○	○	○	○						
14	○	○	○	○	○						
15	○	○	○	○	○						
16	○	○	○	○	○						
17	○	○	○	○	○						
18	○	○	○	○	○						
19	○	○	○	○	○						
20	○	○	○	○	○						

Math

	A B C D E		A B C D E
1	○ ○ ○ ○ ○	21	○ ○ ○ ○ ○
2	○ ○ ○ ○ ○	22	○ ○ ○ ○ ○
3	○ ○ ○ ○ ○	23	○ ○ ○ ○ ○
4	○ ○ ○ ○ ○	24	○ ○ ○ ○ ○
5	○ ○ ○ ○ ○	25	○ ○ ○ ○ ○
6	○ ○ ○ ○ ○	26	○ ○ ○ ○ ○
7	○ ○ ○ ○ ○	27	○ ○ ○ ○ ○
8	○ ○ ○ ○ ○	28	○ ○ ○ ○ ○
9	○ ○ ○ ○ ○	29	○ ○ ○ ○ ○
10	○ ○ ○ ○ ○	30	○ ○ ○ ○ ○
11	○ ○ ○ ○ ○		
12	○ ○ ○ ○ ○		
13	○ ○ ○ ○ ○		
14	○ ○ ○ ○ ○		
15	○ ○ ○ ○ ○		
16	○ ○ ○ ○ ○		
17	○ ○ ○ ○ ○		
18	○ ○ ○ ○ ○		
19	○ ○ ○ ○ ○		
20	○ ○ ○ ○ ○		

Reading Comprehension

Directions: The following questions are based on several reading passages. A series of questions follow each passage. Read each passage carefully, and then answer the questions based on it. You may reread the passage as often as you wish. When you have finished answering the questions based on one passage, go right onto the next passage. Choose the best answer based on the information given and implied.

Questions 1 – 4 refer to the following passage.

Passage 1 - The Life of Helen Keller

Many people have heard of Helen Keller. She is famous because she was unable to see or hear, but learned to speak and read and went onto attend college and earn a degree. Her life is a very interesting story, one that she developed into an autobiography, which was then adapted into both a stage play and a movie. How did Helen Keller overcome her disabilities to become a famous woman? Read on to find out. Helen Keller was not born blind and deaf. When she was a small baby, she had a very high fever for several days. As a result of her sudden illness, baby Helen lost her eyesight and her hearing. Because she was so young when she went deaf and blind, Helen Keller never had any recollection of being able to see or hear. Since she could not hear, she could not learn to talk. Since she could not see, it was difficult for her to move around. For the first six years of her life, her world was very still and dark.

Imagine what Helen's childhood was like. She could not hear her mother's voice. She could not see the beauty of her parent's farm. She could not recognize who was giving her a hug, or a bath or even where her bedroom was each night. Sadly, she could not communicate with her parents in any way. She could not express her feelings or tell them the things she wanted. It must have been a very sad childhood.

When Helen was six years old, her parents hired her a teacher named Anne Sullivan. Anne was a young woman who was almost blind. However, she could hear and she could read Braille, so she was a perfect teacher for young Helen. At first, Anne had a very hard time teaching Helen anything. She described her first impression of Helen as a "wild thing, not a child." Helen did not like Anne at first either. She bit and hit Anne when Anne tried to teach her. However, the two of them eventually came to have a great deal of love and respect.

Anne taught Helen to hear by putting her hands on people's throats. She could feel the sounds people made. In time, Helen learned to feel what people said. Next, Anne taught Helen to read Braille, which is how books are written for the blind. Finally, Anne taught Helen to talk. Although Helen did learn to talk, it was hard for anyone but Anne to understand her.

As Helen grew older, she amazed more and more people with her story. She went to college and wrote books about her life. She gave talks to the public, with Anne at her side, translating her words. Today, both Anne Sullivan and Helen Keller are famous women who are respected for their lives' work.

1. Helen Keller could not see and hear and so, what was her biggest problem in childhood?

    a. Inability to communicate

    b. Inability to walk

    c. Inability to play

    d. Inability to eat

2. Helen learned to hear by feeling the vibrations people made when they spoke. What were these vibrations were felt through?

    a. Mouth
    b. Throat
    c. Ears
    d. Lips

3. From the passage, we can infer that Anne Sullivan was a patient teacher. We can infer this because

    a. Helen hit and bit her and Anne remained her teacher.
    b. Anne taught Helen to read only.
    c. Anne was hard of hearing too.
    d. Anne wanted to be a teacher.

4. Helen Keller learned to speak but Anne translated her words when she spoke in public. The reason Helen needed a translator was because

    a. Helen spoke another language.
    b. Helen's words were hard for people to understand.
    c. Helen spoke very quietly.
    d. Helen did not speak but only used sign language.

Questions 5 – 7 refer to the following passage.

Passage 2 - Ways Characters Communicate in Theater

Playwrights give their characters voices in a way that gives depth and added meaning to what happens on stage during their play. There are different types of speech in scripts that allow characters to talk with themselves, with other characters, and even with the audience.

It is very unique to theater that characters may talk "to themselves." When characters do this, the speech they give is called a soliloquy. Soliloquies are usually poetic, introspective, moving, and can tell audience members about the feelings, motivations, or suspicions of an individual character without that character having to reveal them to other characters on stage. "To be or not to be" is a famous soliloquy given by Hamlet as he considers difficult but important themes, such as life and death.

The most common type of communication in plays is when one character is speaking to another or a group of other characters. This is generally called dialogue, but can also be called monologue if one character speaks without being interrupted for a long time. It is not necessarily the most important type of communication, but it is the most common because the plot of the play cannot really progress without it.

Lastly, and most unique to theater (although it has been used somewhat in film) is when a character speaks directly to the audience. This is called an aside, and scripts usually specifically direct actors to do this. Asides are usually comical, an inside joke between the character and the audience, and very short. The actor will usually face the audience when delivering them, even if it's for a moment, so the audience can recognize this move as an aside.

All three of these types of communication are important to the art of theater, and have been perfected by famous playwrights like Shakespeare. Understanding these types of communication can help an audience member grasp what is artful about the script and action of a play.

5. According to the passage, characters in plays communicate to

      a. move the plot forward

      b. show the private thoughts and feelings of one character

      c. make the audience laugh

      d. add beauty and artistry to the play

6. When Hamlet delivers "To be or not to be," he can be described as

    a. solitary

    b. thoughtful

    c. dramatic

    d. hopeless

7. The author uses parentheses to punctuate "although it has been used somewhat in film,"

    a. to show that films are less important

    b. instead of using commas so that the sentence is not interrupted

    c. because parenthesis help separate details that are not as important

    d. to show that films are not as artistic

Questions 8 – 10 refer to the following passage.

Passage 3 - Low Blood Sugar

As the name suggest, low blood sugar is low sugar levels in the bloodstream. This can occur when you have not eaten properly and undertake strenuous activity, or, when you are very hungry. When Low blood sugar occurs regularly and is ongoing, it is a medical condition called hypoglycaemia. This condition can occur in diabetics and in healthy adults.

Causes of low blood sugar can include excessive alcohol consumption, metabolic problems, stomach surgery, pancreas, liver or kidneys problems, as well as a side-effect of some medications.

Symptoms

There are different symptoms depending on the severity of the case.

Mild hypoglycaemia can lead to feelings of nausea and hunger. The patient may also feel nervous, jittery and have fast heart beats. Sweaty skin, clammy and cold skin are likely symptoms.
Moderate hypoglycaemia can result in a short temper, confusion, nervousness, fear and blurring of vision. The patient may feel weak and unsteady.

Severe cases of hypoglycaemia can lead to seizures, coma, fainting spells, nightmares, headaches, excessive sweats and severe tiredness.

Diagnosis of low blood sugar

A doctor can diagnosis this medical condition by asking the patient questions and testing blood and urine samples. Home testing kits are available for patients to monitor blood sugar levels. It is important to see a qualified doctor though. A doctor can test to safely rule out other medical conditions that could affect blood sugar levels.

Treatment

Quick treatments include drinking or eating foods and drinks with high sugar contents. Good examples include soda, fruit juice, hard candy and raisins. Glucose energy tablets can also help. Doctors may also recommend medications and well as changes in diet and exercise routine to treat chronic low blood sugar.

8. Based on the article, which of the following is true?

    a. Low blood sugar can happen to anyone.

    b. Low blood sugar only happens to diabetics.

    c. Low blood sugar can occur even.

    d. None of the statements are true.

9. Which of the following are the author's opinion?

a. Quick treatments include drinking or eating foods and drinks with high sugar contents.

b. None of the statements are opinions.

c. This condition can occur in diabetics and in healthy adults.

d. There are different symptoms depending on the severity of the case

10. What is the author's purpose?

a. To inform

b. To persuade

c. To entertain

d. To analyze

11. Which of the following is not a detail?

a. A doctor can diagnosis this medical condition by asking the patient questions and testing.

b. A doctor will test blood and urine samples.

c. Glucose energy tablets can also help.

d. Home test kits monitor blood sugar levels.

d. None of the above.

Questions 12 – 15 refer to the following passage.

How To Get A Good Nights Sleep

Sleep is just as essential for healthy living as water, air and food. Sleep allows the body to rest and replenish depleted energy levels. Sometimes we may for various reasons have trouble sleeping which has a serious effect on our health. Those who have prolonged sleeping problems are facing a serious medical condition and should see a qualified doctor when possible for help. Here is simple guide that can help you sleep better at night.

Try to create a natural pattern of waking up and sleeping around the same time every day - avoid going to bed too early and sleeping past your usual wake up time. Going to bed and getting up at radically different times everyday confuses your body clock. Try to establish a natural rhythm as much as you can.

Exercises and a bit of physical activity can help you sleep better at night. If you are having problem sleeping, try to be as active as you can during the day. If you are tired from physical activity, falling asleep is a natural and easy process for your body. If you remain inactive during the day, you will find it harder to sleep properly at night. Try walking, jogging, swimming or simple stretches close to your bed time.

Afternoon naps are great to refresh you during the day, but they may also keep you awake at night. If you feel sleepy during the day, get up, take a walk and get busy to keep from sleeping. Stretching is a good way to increase blood flow to the brain and keep you alert so that you don't sleep during the day. This will help you sleep better night.

> A warm bath or a glass of milk in the evening can help your body relax and prepare for sleep. A cold bath will wake you up and keep you up for several hours. Also avoid eating too late before bed.

12. How would you describe this sentence?

    a. A recommendation

    b. An opinion

    c. A fact

    d. A diagnosis

13. Which of the following is an alternative title for this article?

    a. Exercise and a good night's sleep

    b. Benefits of a good night's sleep

    c. Tips for a good night's sleep

    d. Lack of sleep is a serious medical condition

14. Which of the following cannot be inferred from this article?

    a. Biking is helpful for getting a good night's sleep

    b. Mental activity is helpful for getting a good night's sleep

    c. Eating bedtime snacks is not recommended

    d. Getting up at the same time is helpful for a good night's sleep

15. What is a disadvantage of taking naps?

    a. They may keep you awake.

    b. There are no disadvantages

    c. They may help you sleep better

    d. They may affect your diet

Question 16 refers to the following Table of Contents.

Contents

    Science Self-assessment 81
    Answer Key 91
    Science Tutorials 96
    Scientific Method 96
    Biology 99
    Heredity: Genes and Mutation 104
    Classification 108

Ecology 110
Chemistry 112
Energy: Kinetic and Mechanical 126
Energy: Work and Power 130
Force: Newton's Three Laws 132

16. Consider the table of contents above. What page would you find information about natural selection and adaptation?

    a. 81

    b. 90

    c. 110

    d. 132

Questions 17 – 20 refer to the following passage.

Passage 5 - Pearl Harbor

In 1941, the world was at war. The United States was trying to stay out of the conflict. In Europe, the countries of Germany and Italy had formed an alliance to expand their land and territory. Germany had already taken over Poland, Denmark, and parts of France. They were heading next toward England and due to all the fighting in Europe, there were battles taking place as far south as North Africa, where the German and Italian armies were fighting the British.

This got even worse when the Asian nation of Japan formed an alliance with Germany and Italy. Together, the three countries called themselves, the AXIS. Now, the war was in the Pacific as well as in Europe and Northern Africa. Many Americans thought that perhaps now was the time for the United States to join with its ally, Great Britain and stop the Axis from taking over more regions of the world.

In 1941, Franklin Roosevelt was President of the United States. His fear at the time was that Japan would try to take over many countries in Asia. He did not want to see that happen, so he moved some of the United States warships that had been stationed in San Diego, to the military base at Pearl Harbor, in Honolulu, Hawaii.

Japan quietly plotted their attack. They waited until the early hours of the morning on Sunday, December 7, 1941. Then, 350 Japanese war plans began to drop bombs on the U.S. ships at Pearl Harbor. The first bombs fell at 7:48 a.m. and only 90 minutes later, the attack was over. Pearl Harbor was decimated. 8 battleships were damaged. Eleven ships were sunk and 300 U.S. planes were destroyed. Most devastating was the loss of life 2,400 U.S. military members was killed in the attack and 1,282 were injured.

President Roosevelt addressed the country via the radio and said "Today is a day that will live in infamy." He asked Congress to declare war on Japan. War was declared on Japan on December 8th and on Germany and Italy on December 11th. The United States had entered World War Two.

17. After reading the passage, what can we infer infamy means?

    a. Famous

    b. Remembered in a good way

    c. Remembered in a bad way

    d. Easily forgotten

18. What three countries formed the Axis?

    a. Italy, England, Germany

    b. United States, England, Italy

    c. Germany, Japan, Italy

    d. Germany, Japan, United States

19. What do you think was President Roosevelt's reason for moving warships to Pearl Harbor?

    a. He feared Japan would bomb San Diego

    b. He knew Japan was going to attack Pearl Harbor

    c. He was planning to attack Japan

    d. He wanted to try to protect Asian countries from Japanese takeover

20. Why do you think Japan chose a Sunday morning at 7:48 am for their attack?

    a. They knew the military slept late

    b. There is a law against bombing countries on a Sunday

    c. They wanted the attack to catch people by surprise

    d. That was the only free time they had to attack.

Questions 21 - 24 refer to the following recipe.

If You Have Allergies, You're Not Alone

People who experience allergies might joke that their immune systems have let them down or are seriously lacking. Truthfully though, people who experience allergic reactions or allergy symptoms during certain times of the year have heightened immune systems that are, "better" than those of people who have perfectly healthy but less militant immune systems.

Still, when a person has an allergic reaction, they are having an adverse reaction to a substance that is considered normal to most people. Mild allergic reactions usually have symptoms like itching, runny nose, red eyes, or bumps or discoloration of the skin. More serious allergic reactions, such as those to animal and insect poisons or certain foods, may result in the closing of the throat, swelling of the eyes, low blood pressure, inability to breath, and can even be fatal.

Different treatments help different allergies, depending on the nature and severity of the allergy. It is recommended to patients with severe allergies to take extra precautions, such as carrying an EpiPen, which treats anaphylactic shock and may prevent death, always in order for the remedy to be readily available and more effective. When an allergy is not so severe, treatments may be used just relieve a person of uncomfortable symptoms. Over the counter allergy medicines treat milder symptoms, and can be bought at any grocery store and used in moderation to help people with allergies live normally.

There are many tests available to assess whether a person has allergies or what they may be allergic to, and advances in these tests and the medicine used to treat patients continues to improve. Despite this fact, allergies still affect many people throughout the year or even every day. Medicines used to treat allergies have side-effects, and it is difficult to bring the body into balance with the use of medicine. Regardless, many of those who live with allergies are grateful for what is available and find it useful in maintaining their lifestyles.

21. According to this passage, which group does the word "militant" belong in

    a. sickly, ailing, faint

    b. strength, power, vigor

    c. active, fighting, warring

    d. worn, tired, breaking down

22. The author says that "medicines used to treat allergies have side-effects of their own" to

    a. point out that doctors aren't very good at diagnosing and treating allergies

    b. argue that because of the large number of people with allergies, a cure will never be found

    c. explain that allergy medicines aren't cures, and some compromise must be made

    d. argue that more wholesome remedies should be researched and medicines banned

23. It can be inferred that _____ recommend that some people with allergies carry medicine with them.

   a. the author
   b. doctors
   c. the makers of EpiPen
   d. people with allergies

24. The author has written this passage to

   a. inform readers on symptoms of allergies so people with allergies can get help
   b. persuade readers to be proud of having allergies
   c. inform readers on different remedies so people with allergies receive the right help
   d. describe different types of allergies, their symptoms, and their remedies

Questions 25 – 26 refer to the following email.

SUBJECT: MEDICAL STAFF CHANGES

To all staff:

This email is to advise you of a paper on recommended medical staff changes has been posted to the Human Resources website.

The contents are of primary interest to medical staff, other staff may be interested in reading it, particularly those in medical support roles.

The paper deals with several major issues:

   1. Improving our ability to attract top quality staff to the hospital, and retain our existing staff. These changes will make our position and departmental names internationally recognizable and comparable with North American and North Asian departments and positions.

2. Improving our ability to attract top quality staff by introducing greater flexibility in the departmental structure.

3. General comments on issues to be further discussed relative to research staff.

The changes outlined in this paper are significant. I encourage you to read the document and send to me any comments you may have, so that it can be enhanced and improved.

Gordon Simms
Administrator,
Seven Oaks Regional Hospital

25. Are all hospital staff required to read the document posted to the Human Resources website?

    a. Yes all staff are required to read the document.

    b. No, reading the document is optional.

    c. Only medical staff are required to read the document.

    d. none of the above are correct.

26. Have the changes to medical staff been made?

    a. Yes, the changes have been made.

    b. No, the changes are only being discussed.

    c. Some of the changes have been made.

    d. None of the choices are correct.

Questions 27 – 30 refer to the following passage.

When a Poet Longs to Mourn, He Writes an Elegy

Poems are an expressive, especially emotional, form of writing. They have been in literature virtually from the time civilizations invented the written word. Poets often portrayed as moody, secluded, and even troubled, but this is because poets are introspective and feel deeply about the current events and cultural norms they are surrounded with. Poets often produce the most telling literature, giving insight into the society and mind-set they come from. This can be done in many forms.
The oldest types of poems often include many stanzas, which may or may not rhyme, and are more about telling a story than experimenting with language or words. The most common types of ancient poetry are epics, which are usually extremely long stories that follow a hero through his journey, or ellegies, which are often solemn in tone and used to mourn or lament something or someone. The Mesopotamians are often said to have invented the written word, and their literature is among the oldest in the world, including the epic poem titled "Epic of Gilgamesh." Similar in style and length to "Gilgamesh" is "Beowulf," an ellegy written in Old English and set in Scandinavia. These poems are often used by professors as the earliest examples of literature.

The importance of poetry was revived in the Renaissance. At this time, Europeans discovered the style and beauty of ancient Greek arts, and poetry was among those. Shakespeare is the most well-known poet of the time, and he used poetry not only to write poems but also to write plays for the theater. The most popular forms of poetry during the Renaissance included villanelles, (a nineteen-line poetic form) sonnets, as well as the epic. Poets during this time focused on style and form, and developed very specific rules and outlines for how an exceptional poem should be written.

As often happens in the arts, modern poets have rejected the constricting rules of Renaissance poets, and free form poems are much more popular. Some modern poems would read just like stories if they weren't arranged into lines and stanzas. It is difficult to tell which poems and poets will be the most important, because works of art often become more famous in hindsight, after the poet has died and society can look at itself without being in the moment. Modern poetry continues to develop, and will no doubt continue to change as values, thought, and writing continue to change.

Poems can be among the most enlightening and uplifting texts for a person to read if they are looking to connect with the past, connect with other people, or try to gain an understanding of what is happening in their time.

27. In summary, the author has written this passage

    a. as a foreword that will introduce a poem in a book or magazine

    b. because she loves poetry and wants more people to like it

    c. to give a brief history of poems

    d. to convince students to write poems

28. The author organizes the paragraphs mainly by

    a. moving chronologically, explaining which types of poetry were common in that time

    b. talking about new types of poems each paragraph and explaining them a little

    c. focusing on one poet or group of people and the poems they wrote

    d. explaining older types of poetry so she can talk about modern poetry

29. The author's claim that poetry has been around "virtually from the time civilizations invented the written word" is supported by the detail that

    a. Beowulf is written in Old English, which is not really in use any longer

    b. epic poems told stories about heroes

    c. the Renaissance poets tried to copy Greek poets

    d. the Mesopotamians are credited with both inventing the word and writing "Epic of Gilgamesh"

30. According to the passage, the word "telling" means

    a. speaking

    b. significant

    c. soothing

    d. wordy

Memory

Directions: You have five minutes to memorize the following information. Do not write anything down. Questions follow on page 163.

Name: William Jackson

Description: 5'11" Caucasian male. Brown hair with receding hairline. Slight build. No identifying marks.

Wanted for: Armed Robbery

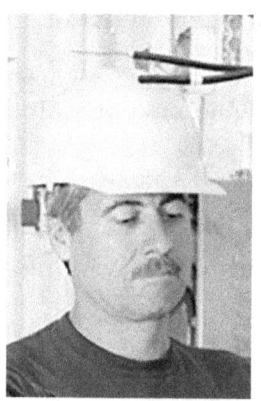

Name: Kenneth Walker

Description: 5 ft. Caucasian male with heavy build. Small scar on right forehead.

Wanted for: Armed robbery

Make: Porche Carrera

Color: White

License: Manitoba APT 936

Wanted for: Dangerous Driving

Make: Smart Car

Color: White

License: New Brunswick CPV 439

Wanted for: Criminal Harassment

Name: Steven Hermandez

Description: 6 ft Latino male with tattoos on both arms and chest.

Wanted For: Theft of motor vehicle

Name: Linda Moore

Description: 5' 4" Caucasian female, blonde hair, brown eyes, tattoos on left forearm

Wanted For: Shoplifting

Make: Volkwagen Passat

Color: White

License: British Columbia AG5 26C

Wanted for: Sexual Assault

Make: Volkwagen Beetle

Color: Yellow

License: AG5 26C

Wanted for: Sexual Assault

MEMORY QUESTIONS

Directions: Answer questions 1 - 7 based on the information given on above.

1. **What identifying marks does Kenneth Walker have?**

    a. Scar on forehead

    b. Tattoo on chest

    c. Tattoo on right arm

    d. No identifying marks

2. **What is Kenneth Walker wanted for?**

    a. Dangerous Driving

    b. Armed Robbery

    c. Fraud

    d. Criminal Harassment

3. **Which car is wanted for Dangerous Driving?**

    a. Porche Carrera

    b. Smart Car

    c. Volkwagen Passat

    d. None of the above.

4. **What Province is the Smart Car from?**

    a. British Columbia

    b. New Brunswick

    c. Alberta

    d. Ontario

5. What is Steven Hermandez wanted for?

    a. Theft of motor vehicle

    b. Fraud

    c. Armed Robbery

    d. Criminal Harassment

6. What identifying marks does Linda Moore have?

    a. No identifying marks

    b. Scar on forehead

    c. Tattoos on forearm

    d. Scar on upper lip

7. What color is the Volkswagen Beetle?

    a. White

    b. Yellow

    c. Red

    d. Blue

ENGLISH

1. Choose a verb that means fearless or invulnerable to intimidation and fear.

    a. Feeble

    b. Strongest

    c. Dauntless

    d. Super

2. Choose a word that means the same as the underlined word.

I see the differences when they are placed side-by-side and <u>juxtaposed.</u>

    a. Compared
    b. Eliminated
    c. Overturned
    d. Exonerated

3. Choose the best definition of regicide.

    a. v. To endow or furnish with requisite ability, character, knowledge and skill
    b. n. killing of a king
    c. adj. Disposed to seize by violence or by unlawful or greedy methods
    d. v. To refresh after labor

4. Choose the best definition of pernicious.

    a. Deadly
    b. Infectious
    c. Common
    d. Rare

5. Fill in the blank.

After she received her influenza vaccination, Nan thought that she was _____ to the common cold.

    a. Immune
    b. Susceptible
    c. Vulnerable
    d. At risk

6. Choose a word that means the same as the underlined word.

She performed the gymnastics and stretches so well! I have never seen anyone so <u>nimble</u>.

    a. Awkward

    b. Agile

    c. Quick

    d. Taut

7. Choose a word that means the same as the underlined word.

Are there any more <u>queries</u>? We have already had so many questions today.

    a. Questions

    b. Commands

    c. Obfuscations

    d. Paradoxes

8. Choose a verb that means to remove a leader or high official from position.

    a. Sack

    b. Suspend

    c. Depose

    d. Dropped

9. Choose the best definition of pedestrian.

    a. Rare

    b. Often

    c. Walking or Running

    d. Commonplace

10. Choose the best definition of petulant.

   a. Patient

   b. Childish

   c. Impatient

   d. Mature

11. Choose the correct spelling.

   a. Humoros

   b. Humouros

   c. Humorous

   d. Humorus

12. Choose the correct spelling.

   a. Knowlege

   b. Knowledge

   c. Knowlegde

   d. Knowlledge

13. Choose the correct spelling.

   a. Camaraderie

   b. Camaredere

   c. Camaradere

   d. Cameraderie

14. Choose the correct spelling.

   a. Mathematics

   b. Mathmatics

   c. Matematics

   d. Mathamatics

15. Choose the correct spelling.

a. Conscentious

b. Conscientios

c. Conscientious

d. Consceintious

16. Choose the correct spelling.

a. Leisuire

b. Lesure

c. Lesure

d. Leisure

17. Choose the correct spelling.

a. Pigeone

b. Pigoen

c. Pigeon

d. Pidgeon

18. Choose the correct spelling.

a. Odyessy

b. Odeyssey

c. Odysey

d. Odyssey

19. Choose the correct spelling.

a. Sacreligious

b. Sacriligious

c. Sacrilegious

d. Sacrilegous

20. Choose the correct spelling.

a. Accommodate
b. Accommodate
c. Acommodate
d. Accommodaite

21. Choose the sentence with the correct capitalization.

a. My favorite Dylan song is blowin' in the wind.
b. My favorite dylan song is Blowin' in the Wind.
c. My favorite Dylan song is Blowin' in the Wind.
d. None of the above.

22. Choose the sentence with the correct capitalization.

a. My latest novel, Danger on the Rhine will be published next year.
b. My latest novel, danger on the Rhine will be published next year.
c. My latest novel, danger on the rhine will be published next year.
d. None of the above.

23. Choose the sentence with the correct usage.

a. The Chinese live in one of the world's most populous nations, while a citizen of Bermuda lives in one of the least populous.
b. The Chinese lives in one of the world's most populous nations, while a citizen of Bermuda live in one of the least populous.
c. The Chinese live in one of the world's most populous nations, while a citizen of Bermuda live in one of the least populous.
d. The Chinese lives in one of the world's most populous nations, while a citizen of Bermuda lives in one of the least populous.

24. Choose the sentence with the correct usage.

a. Disease is highly prevalent in poorer nations; the most dominant disease is malaria.

b. Diseases are highly prevalent in poorer nations; the most dominant disease is malaria.

c. Disease is highly prevalent in poorer nations; the most dominant Diseases are malaria.

d. Diseases are highly prevalent in poorer nations; the most dominant Diseases are malaria.

25. Choose the sentence with the correct usage.

a. Although I would prefer to have dog, I actually own a cat.

b. Although I would prefer to have a dog, I actually own cat.

c. Although I would prefer to have a dog, I actually own a cat.

d. Although I would prefer to have dog, I actually own cat.

26. Choose the sentence with the correct usage.

a. The volunteers brought groceries and toys to the homeless shelter; the latter were given to the staff, while the former were given directly to the children.

b. The volunteers brought groceries and toys to the homeless shelter; the former was given to the staff, while the latter was given directly to the children.

c. The volunteers brought groceries and toys to the homeless shelter; the groceries were given to the staff, while the former was given directly to the children.

d. The volunteers brought groceries and toys to the homeless shelter; the latter was given to the staff, while the groceries were given directly to the children.

27. Choose the sentence with the correct grammar.

a. His doctor suggested that he eat less snacks and do fewer lounging on the couch.

b. His doctor suggested that he eat fewer snacks and do less lounging on the couch.

c. His doctor suggested that he eat less snacks and do less lounging on the couch.

d. His doctor suggested that he eat fewer snacks and do fewer lounging on the couch.

28. Choose the sentence with the correct grammar.

a. However, I believe that he didn't really try that hard.

b. However I believe that he didn't really try that hard.

c. However; I believe that he didn't really try that hard.

d. However: I believe that he didn't really try that hard.

29. Choose the sentence with the correct grammar.

a. There was however, very little difference between the two.

b. There was, however very little difference between the two.

c. There was; however, very little difference between the two.

d. There was, however, very little difference between the two.

30. Choose the sentence with the correct grammar.

a. Don would never have thought of that book, but you could have reminded him.

b. Don would never of thought of that book, but you could have reminded him.

c. Don would never have thought of that book, but you could of have reminded him.

d. Don would never of thought of that book, but you could of reminded him.

Mathematics

1. What is 1/3 of 3/4?

    a. 1/4
    b. 1/3
    c. 2/3
    d. 3/4

2. What fraction of $1500 is $75?

    a. 1/14
    b. 3/5
    c. 7/10
    d. 1/20

3. 3.14 + 2.73 + 23.7 =

    a. 28.57
    b. 30.57
    c. 29.56
    d. 29.57

4. A woman spent 15% of her income on an item and ends with $120. What percentage of her income is left?

    a. 12%
    b. 85%
    c. 75%
    d. 95%

5. A mother is making spaghetti for her son. The recipe that she's using says that for 500 grams of spaghetti, she should add 0.75 grams of salt. However, the mom just wants 125 grams of spaghetti. Based on this information, how much salt should she use?

    a. 0.38 grams
    b. 0.75 grams
    c. 0.19 grams
    d. 0.25 grams

6. A pet store sold $19,304.56 worth of merchandise in June. If the cost of products sold was $5,284.34, employees were paid $8,384.76, and rent was $2,920.00, how much profit did the store make in June?

    a. $5,635.46
    b. $2,715.46
    c. $14,020.22
    d. $10,019.80

7. At the beginning of 2009, Madalyn invested $5,000 in a savings account. The account pays 4% interest per year. At the end of the year, after the interest was awarded, how much did Madalyn have in the account?

    a. $5,200
    b. $5,020
    c. $5,110
    d. $7,000

8. If 144 students need to go on a trip and the buses each carry 36 students, how many buses are needed?

    a. 6
    b. 5
    c. 4
    d. 3

9. If a square if five feet tall, what is its area?

  a. 5 square feet
  b. 10 square feet
  c. 20 square feet
  d. 25 square feet

10. With a purely random guess, what are the chances of correctly guessing the month in which a person was born?

  a. 1 : 3
  b. 1 : 6
  c. 1 : 4
  d. 1 : 12

11. John is a barber and receives 40% of the amount paid by each of his customers. John gets all tips paid to him. If a man pays $8.50 for a haircut and pays a tip of $1.30, how much money goes to John?

  a. $3.92
  b. $4.70
  c. $5.30
  d. $6.40

12. Susan was surprised to find she had two more quarters than she believed she had in her purse. If quarters are the only coins, and the total is $8.75, how many quarters did she think she had?

  a. 35
  b. 29
  c. 31
  d. 33

13. There were some oranges in a basket, by adding 8/5 of these, the total became 130. How many oranges were in the basket?

   a. 60
   b. 50
   c. 40
   d. 35

14. Mr. Brown bought 5 burgers, 3 drinks, 4 fries for his family and a cookie for the dog. If the price of all single items is same, at $1.30 and a 3.5% tax is added, then what is the total cost of dinner?

   a. $16.00
   b. $16.90
   c. $17.00
   d. $17.50

15. A distributor purchased 550 kilograms of potatoes for $165. He distributed these at a rate of $6.4 per 20 kilograms to 15 shops, $3.4 per 10 kilograms to 12 shops and the remainder at $1.8 per 5 kilograms. If his total distribution cost is $10, what will his profit be?

   a. $10.40
   b. $8.60
   c. $14.90
   d. $23.40

16. Convert 3 yards to feet

   a. 18 feet
   b. 12 feet
   c. 9 feet
   d. 27 feet

17. 12t - 10 = 14t + 2. Find t

  a. -6
  b. -4
  c. 4
  d. 6

18. The price of a book went up from $20 to $25. What percent did the price increase?

  a. 5%
  b. 10%
  c. 20%
  d. 25%

19. The price of a book decreased from $25 to $20. What percent did the price decrease?

  a. 5%
  b. 10%
  c. 20%
  d. 25%

20. 305 X 25 =

  a. 6525
  b. 7625
  c. 5026
  d. 7026

21. $(x^2 - 2)(3x^2 - 3x + 7) =$

  a. $3x^3 - 3x^3 + x^2 + 4x - 12$
  b. $3x^4 - 3x^3 + x^2 + 6x - 14$
  c. $3x^2 - 3x^3 + x + 6x - 10$
  d. $3x^2 - 3x + x + 4x - 14$

22. Solve the system: 4x - y = 5; x + 2y = 8

   a. (3, 2)
   b. (3, 3)
   c. (2, 3)
   d. (2, 2)

23. Find 2 numbers whose difference is 11 and product is -24. (There is more than one solution.)

   a. (3,-8)
   b. (-3,8)
   c. (-3,-8)
   d. (3,8)

24. Driver B drove his car 20 km/h faster than the driver A, and the driver B traveled 480 km 2 hours before driver A. What was the speed of the driver A?

   a. 70
   b. 80
   c. 60
   d. 90

25. If x = √7 - 1 and y = √7 + 1, find the value of (x + y) / (x - y).

   a. -√7
   b. -2
   c. 2
   d. √7

26. Solve the linear equation:
   $-x - 7 = -3x - 9$

   a. -1
   b. 0
   c. 1
   d. 2

27. 6 workers of the same capacity begin building a wall. Every day, one worker leaves, and the total job is completed in 4 days. If none of the workers left the job, how many days would it take to complete the wall?

   a. 1
   b. 1.5
   c. 2
   d. 3

28. Find the result of the operation
$(\sqrt{75} - 3\sqrt{48}) / \sqrt{147} + \sqrt{20}$ by simplification and approximation and then rounding the result to tenths digit.

   a. -4.4
   b. 3.4
   c. -2.8
   d. 3.2

29. $\sqrt[4]{2 * \sqrt[3]{4}} * \sqrt[3]{\sqrt{8}} = \sqrt[6]{4 * \sqrt[2]{2^{x+1}}}$ is given. Find the value of x.

   a. 2
   b. 3
   c. 5
   d. 6

30. ((1 - 1/3) * (1 + 1/5)) / (1/8 * 4/5 - 1/3) =

    a. -24/7
    b. -7/24
    c. 7/24
    d. 24/7

Answer Key

Reading Comprehension

1. A
The correct answer because that fact is stated directly in the passage. The passage explains that Anne taught Helen to hear by allowing her to feel the vibrations in her throat.

2. B
We can infer that Anne is a patient teacher because she did not leave or lose her temper when Helen bit or hit her; she just kept trying to teach Helen. Choice B is incorrect because Anne taught Helen to read and talk. Choice C is incorrect because Anne could hear. She was partially blind, not deaf. Choice D is incorrect because it does not have to do with patience.

3. A
The passage states that it was hard for anyone but Anne to understand Helen when she spoke. Choice A is incorrect because the passage does not mention Helen spoke a foreign language. Choice C is incorrect because there is no mention of how quiet or loud Helen's voice was. Choice D is incorrect because we know from reading the passage that Helen did learn to speak.

4. B
This question tests the reader's summarization skills. The other choices A, B, and C focus on portions of the second paragraph that are too narrow and do not relate to the specific portion of text in question. The complexity of the sentence may mislead students into selecting one of these answers, but rearranging or restating the sentence will lead the reader to the correct answer. In addition, choice A makes an assumption that may or may not be true about the intentions of the company, choice B focuses on one product rather than the idea of the products, and choice C makes an assumption about women that may or may not be true and is not supported by the text.

5. D
This question tests the reader's summarization skills. The question is asking very generally about the message of the passage, and the title, "Ways Characters Communicate in Theater," is one indication of that. The other choices A, B, and C are all directly from the text, and therefore readers may be inclined to select one of them, but are too specific to encapsulate the entirety of the passage and its message.

6. B
The paragraph on soliloquies mentions "To be or not to be," and it is from the context of that paragraph that readers may understand that because "To be or not to be" is a soliloquy, Hamlet will be introspective, or thoughtful, while delivering it. It is true that actors deliver soliloquies alone, and may be "solitary" (choice A), but "thoughtful" (choice B) is more true to the overall idea of the paragraph. Readers may choose C because drama and theater can be used interchangeably and the passage mentions that soliloquies are unique to theater (and therefore drama), but this answer is not specific enough to the paragraph in question. Readers may pick up on the theme of life and death and Hamlet's true intentions and select that he is "hopeless" (choice D), but those themes are not discussed either by this paragraph or passage, as a close textual reading and analysis confirms.

7. C
This question tests the reader's grammatical skills. Choice B seems logical, but parenthesis are actually considered to be a stronger break in a sentence than commas are, and along this line of thinking, actually disrupt the sentence more.

Choices A and D make comparisons between theater and film that are not made in the passage, and may or may not be true. This detail does clarify the statement that asides are most unique to theater by adding that it is not completely unique to theater, which may have been why the author didn't chose not to delete it and instead used parentheses to designate the detail's importance (choice C).

8. A
Low blood sugar occurs both in diabetics and healthy adults.

9. B
None of the statements are the author's opinion.

10. A
The author's purpose is the inform.

11. A
The only statement that is not a detail is, "A doctor can diagnosis this medical condition by asking the patient questions and testing."

12. A
This sentence is a recommendation.

13. C
Tips for a good night's sleep is the best alternative title for this article.

14. B
Mental activity is helpful for a good night's sleep is cannot be inferred from this article.

15. A
From the passage, one disadvantage of taking naps is they may keep you awake at night.

16. A
Based on the partial table of contents, this book is most likely about how to answer multiple choice.

17. C
To be infamous means to be remembered for an evil or terrible action. Therefore, the word infamy means to remember a bad or terrible thing. Choice A is incorrect because being famous is not the same as being infamous. Choice B is incorrect because the attack on Pearl Harbour was not good. Choice D is incorrect because Pearl Harbour was not forgotten.

18. C
Each answer choice except choice C contains the name of at least one country that was not part of the AXIS powers.

19. D

It is stated in the passage. Choice A is not correct because there was no indication that Japan would attack San Diego. Choice B is incorrect because the attack on Pearl Harbor was a surprise. Choice C is incorrect because Roosevelt was not planning to attack Japan.

20. C

The passage clearly states that Japan planned a surprise attack. They chose that early time to catch the U.S. military off guard. Choice A is incorrect because the military does not sleep late. Choice B is incorrect because there is no law against bombing countries. Choice D is incorrect because it makes no sense.

21. C

This question tests the reader's vocabulary skills. The uses of the negatives "but" and "less," especially right next to each other, may confuse readers into answering with choices A or D, which list words that are antonyms to "militant." Readers may also be confused by the comparison of healthy people with what is being described as an overly healthy person-- both people are good, but the reader may look for which one is "worse" in the comparison, and therefore stray toward the antonym words. One key to understanding the meaning of "militant" if the reader is unfamiliar with it is to look at the root of the word; readers can then easily associate it with "military" and gain a sense of what the word signifies: defence (especially considered that the immune system defends the body). Choice C is correct over choice B because "militant" is an adjective, just as the words in choice C are, whereas the words in choice B are nouns.

22. C

This question tests the reader's understanding of function within writing. The other choices are details included surrounding the quoted text, and may therefore confuse the reader. A somewhat contradicts what is said earlier in the paragraph, which is that tests and treatments are improving, and probably doctors are along with them, but the paragraph doesn't actually mention doctors, and the subject of the question is the medicine. Choice B may seem correct to readers who aren't careful to understand that, while the author does mention the large number of people affected, the author is touching on the realities of living with allergies, rather than the likelihood of curing all allergies. Similarly, while the author does mention the "balance" of the body, which is easily associated with "wholesome," the author is not really making an argument and especially is not making an extreme statement that allergy medicines should be outlawed. Again, because the article's tone is on living with allergies, choice C is an appropriate choice that fits with the title and content of the text.

23. B
This question tests the reader's inference skills. The text does not state who is doing the recommending, but the use of the "patients," as well as the general context of the passage, lends itself to the logical partner, "doctors," choice B. The author does mention the recommendation but doesn't present it as her own (i.e. "I recommend that"), so choice A may be eliminated. It may seem plausible that people with allergies (choice D) may recommend medicines or products to other people with allergies, but the text does not necessarily support this interaction taking place. Choice C may be selected because the EpiPen is specifically mentioned, but the use of the phrase "such as" when it is introduced is not limiting enough to assume the recommendation is coming from its creators.

24. D
This question tests the reader's global understanding of the text. Choice D includes the main topics of the three body paragraphs, and isn't too focused on a specific aspect or quote from the text, as the other questions are, giving a skewed summary of what the author intended. The reader may be drawn to choice B because of the title of the passage and the use of words like "better," but the message of the passage is larger and more general than this.

25. B
Reading the document posted to the Human Resources website is optional.

26. B
The document is recommended changes and have not be implemented yet.

27. C

This question tests the reader's summarization skills. The use of the word "actually" in describing what kind of people poets are, as well as other moments like this, may lead readers to selecting choices B or D, but the author is more informational than trying to persuade readers. The author gives no indication that she loves poetry (choice B) or that people, students specifically (D), should write poems. Choice A is incorrect because the style and content of this paragraph do not match those of a foreword; forewords usually focus on the history or ideas of a specific poem to introduce it more fully and help it stand out against other poems. The author here focuses on several poems and gives broad statements. Instead, she tells a kind of story about poems, giving three very broad time periods in which to discuss them, thereby giving a brief history of poetry, as choice C states.

28. A

This question tests the reader's summarization skills. Key words in the topic sentences of each of the paragraphs ("oldest," "Renaissance," "modern") should give the reader an idea that the author is moving chronologically. The opening and closing sentence-paragraphs are broad and talk generally. B seems reasonable, but epic poems are mentioned in two paragraphs, eliminating the idea that only new types of poems are used in each paragraph. Choice C is also easily eliminated because the author clearly mentions several different poets, groups of people, and poems. Choice D also seems reasonable, considering that the author does move from older forms of poetry to newer forms, but use of "so (that)" makes this statement false, for the author gives no indication that she is rushing (the paragraphs are about the same size) or that she prefers modern poetry.

29. D

This question tests the reader's attention to detail. The key word is "invented"--it ties together the Mesopotamians, who invented the written word, and the fact that they, as the inventors, also invented and used poetry. The other selections focus on other details mentioned in the passage, such as that the Renaissance's admiration of the Greeks (choice C) and that Beowulf is in Old English (choice A). Choice B may seem like an attractive answer because it is unlike the others and because the idea of heroes seems rooted in ancient and early civilizations.

30. B
This question tests the reader's vocabulary and contextualization skills. "Telling" is not an unusual word, but it may be used here in a way that is not familiar to readers, as an adjective rather than a verb in gerund form. Choice A may seem like the obvious answer to a reader looking for a verb to match the use they are familiar with. If the reader understands that the word is being used as an adjective and that choice A is a ploy, they may opt to select choice D, "wordy," but it does not make sense in context. Choice C can be easily eliminated, and doesn't have any connection to the paragraph or passage. "Significant" (choice B) makes sense contextually, especially relative to the phrase "give insight" used later in the sentence.

MEMORY

1. D
Kenneth Walker does not have any identifying marks.

2. B
Kenneth Walker is wanted for armed robbery.

3. A
The Porche Carrera is wanted for dangerous driving.

4. B
The Smart Car is from New Brunswick.

5. A
Steven Hermandez is wanted for theft of a motor vehicle.

6. C
Linda Moore has tattoos on her left forearm.

7. B
The Volkwagen Beetle is yellow.

ENGLISH

1. C
Dauntless: adj. Invulnerable to fear or intimidation.

2. A
Juxtaposed: adj. Placed side-by-side, often for comparison or contrast.

3. B
Regicide: v. killing of a king.

4. A
Pernicious: adj. Causing much harm in a subtle way.

5. A
Immune: adj. Resistant to a particular infection or toxin owing to the presence of specific antibodies.

6. B
Nimble: adj. Quick and light in movement or action. Agile.

7. A
Queries: n. Questions or inquiries.

8. C
Depose: To remove (a leader) from (high) office, without killing the incumbent.

9. D
Pedestrian: Ordinary, dull; everyday; unexceptional.

10. B
Petulant: adj. Childishly irritable.

11. C
Humorous is the correct spelling.

12. B
Knowledge is the correct spelling.

13. A
Camaraderie is the correct spelling.

14. A
Mathematics is the correct spelling.

15. C
Conscientious is the correct spelling.

16. D
Leisure is the correct spelling.

17. C
Pigeon is the correct spelling.

18. D
Odyssey is the correct spelling.

19. C
Sacrilegious is the correct spelling.

20. A
Accommodate is the correct spelling.

21. C
The major words in the titles of books, articles, and songs are capitalized. (but not short prepositions or the articles "the," "a," or "an," if they are not the first word of the title)

22. A
Titles of publications are capitalized.

23. A
Singular subjects. "The Chinese" is plural, and "a citizen of Bermuda" is singular.

24. A
Disease is singular.

25. C
Articles of speech. Both dog and cat in this sentence are singular and require the article 'a.'

26. B
Former vs. Latter. 'Former' refers to the first of two things, 'latter' to the second.

27. B
Fewer vs. Less. 'Fewer' is used with countables and 'less' is used with un-countables.

28. A
'However' usage. 'However' usually has a comma before and after.

29. D
'However' Usage. 'However' usually has a comma before and after.

30. A
The third conditional is used for talking about an unreal situation (that did not happen) in the past. For example, "If I had studied harder, [if clause] I would have passed the exam [main clause]. Which is the same as, "I failed the exam, because I didn't study hard enough."

MATHEMATICS

1. A
1/3 X 3/4 = 3/12 = 1/4

2. D
75/1500 = 15/300 = 3/60 = 1/20

3. D
3.14 + 2.73 = 5.87 and 5.87 + 23.7 = 29.57

4. B
Spent 15% - 100% - 15% = 85%

5. C
125 : 500 is the same as 25 : 100 or 1 : 4. So the amount of salt will be 0.75/4 = 0.1875, or about .19 grams.

6. B
Total expenses = 5284.34 + $8,384.76 + $2,920.00 = $16,589.10

Profit = revenue less expenses
$19,304.56 - 16589.10 = $2,715.46

7. A
$5,000 at 4% = 5000 X 4/100
5000 X .4 = 200
So the total after one year will be $5,200

8. C
If each bus carries 36 students, and there are 144 students total, then 144/36 = 4 buses.

9. D
If a square is 5 feet tall, then the area will be 5 X 5 = 25.

10. D
Since there are 12 months in a year = 12 possibilities, the chance of guessing the correct month will be 1 in 12.

11. B
John's total will be 40% of 8.50 plus the tip of $1.30.

8.5 X 4/100 = 8.5 X .4 = 3.40

Total = 3.40 + 1.30 = $4.70.

12. D
If she has $8.75, that will equal 35 quarters. ($8.00 = 32 quarters and $.75 = 3 quarters, total 35 quarters).

She had 2 more quarters than she thought, so she had 35 - 2 = 33 quarters.

13. B
Suppose oranges in the basket before = x, Then: $X + 8x/5 = 130$, $5x + 8x = 650$, so $X = 50$.

14. D
As price of all the single items is same and there are 13 total items. So the total cost will be 13 × 1.3 = $16.90. After 3.5 percent tax this amount will become 16.9×1.035=$17.50.

15. B

The distribution is at three different rates and amounts:

$6.4 per 20 kilograms to 15 shops ... 20•15 = 300 kilograms distributed

$3.4 per 10 kilograms to 12 shops ... 10•12 = 120 kilograms distributed

550 - (300 + 120) = 550 - 420 = 130 kilograms left. This amount is distributed in 5 kilogram portions. So, this means that there are 130/5 = 26 shops.

$1.8 per 130 kilograms.

We need to find the amount he earned overall these distributions.

$6.4 per 20 kilograms : 6.4•15 = $96 for 300 kilograms

$3.4 per 10 kilograms : 3.4•12 = $40.8 for 120 kilograms

$1.8 per 5 kilograms : 1.8•26 = $46.8 for 130 kilograms

So, he earned 96 + 40.8 + 46.8 = $ 183.6

The total cost of distribution is given as $10

The profit is found by: Money earned - money spent ... It is important to remember that he bought 550 kilograms of potatoes for $165 at the beginning:

Profit = 183.6 - 10 - 165 = $8.6

16. C
1 yard = 3 feet, 3 yards = 3 feet x 3 = 9 feet

17. C
12t -10 = 14t + 2

Collect terms with the same variable on the same side, switching to negative if you bring terms over the equals sign.

-2t - 10 = 2

Collect number on the same side switching to negative if you bring terms over the equals sign.

-2t = -8

Divide both sides by -2.
-t = -4
t = 4

18. D
The price increased by $5 ($25-$20). The percent increase is 5/20 x 100 = 5 x 5 = 25%

19. C
The price decreased by $5 ($25-$20). The percent increase = 5/25 x 100 = 5 x 4 = 20%

20. B
305 X 25 = 7625

21. B
$(x^2 - 2)(3x^2 - 3x + 7) = ?$

$= x^2(3x^2 - 3x + 7) - 2(3x^2 - 3x + 7)$

$= x^2(3x^2) + x^2(-3x) + x^2(7) - 2(3x^2) - 2(-3x) - 2(7)$ (6 terms)

$= 3x^4 - 3x^3 + 7x^2 - 6x^2 + 6x - 14$

$= 3x^4 - 3x^3 + (7 - 6)x^2 + 6x - 14$

$= 3x^4 - 3x^3 + x^2 + 6x - 14$

22. C
First, we need to write two equations separately:

4x - y = 5 (I)

x + 2y = 8 (II) ... Here, we can use two ways to solve the system. One is substitution method, the other one is linear elimination method:

1. Substitution Method:

Equation (I) gives us that $y = 4x - 5$. We insert this value of y into equation (II):

$x + 2(4x - 5) = 8$

$x + 8x - 10 = 8$

$9x - 10 = 8$

$9x = 18$

$x = 2$

By knowing $x = 2$, we can find the value of y by inserting $x = 2$ into either of the equations. Choose equation (I):

$4(2) - y = 5$

$8 - y = 5$

$8 - 5 = y$

$y = 3$ → solution is (2, 3)

2. Linear Elimination Method:

2•/ $4x - y = 5$ ... by multiplying equation (I) by 2, we see that -2y will form; and y terms

$x + 2y = 8$ ... will be eliminated when summed with +2y in equation (II):

2•/ $4x - y = 5$

+ $\underline{\ \ \ x + 2y = 8\ \ }$

$8x - 2y = 10$

+ $\underline{\ \ x + 2y = 8\ }$ ... Summing side-by-side:

$8x + x - 2y + 2y = 10 + 8$ ... -2y and +2y cancel

$9x = 18$

x = 2

By knowing x = 2, we can find the value of y by inserting x = 2 into either of the equations. Choose equation (I):

4(2) - y = 5

8 - y = 5

8 - 5 = y

y = 3 → solution is (2, 3)

23. A
Two pieces of information are given, which can be translated into two equations:

x - y = 11 → x = 11 + y

xy = 24

(11+y)y = -24

11y + y² = -24

y² + 11y + 24 = 0

$y_{1,2}$ = (-11 ± √121 - 96)/2

$y_{1,2}$ = (-11 ± √25)/2

$y_{1,2}$ = (-11± 5)/2

y_1 = -8

y_2 = -3

x_1 = 11 + y_1 = 11 - 8 = 3

x_2 = 11 + y_2 = 11 - 3 = 8

24. C

We are told that driver B is 20 km/h faster than driver A. So: V_B = V_A + 20 where V is the velocity. Also, driver B travelled

480 km 2 hours before driver A. So:

x = 480 km

$t_A - 2 = t_B$ where t is the time. Now we know the relationship between drivers A and B in terms of time and velocity. We need to write an equation only depending on V_A (the speed of driver A) which we are asked to find.

Since distance = velocity * time: $480 = V_A * t_A = V_B * t_B$

$480 = (V_A + 20)(t_A - 2)$

$480 = (V_A + 20)(480/V_A - 2)$

$480 = 480 - 2V_A + 20 * 480/V_A - 40$

$0 = -2V_A + 9600/V_A - 40$ ... Multiplying the equation by V_A eliminates the denominator:

$2V_A^2 + 40V_A - 9600 = 0$ ... Simplifying the equation by 2:

$V_A^2 + 20V_A - 4800 = 0$

$V_{A\,1,2} = [-20 \pm \sqrt{(400 + 4 * 4800)}] / 2$

$V_{A1,2} = [-20 \pm 140] / 2$

$V_A = [-20 - 140]/2 = -80$ km/h and $V_A = [-20 + 140]/2 = 60$ km/h

We need to check our answers. It is easy to make a table:

t_A	V_A	V_B	t_B	$t_A - t_B$
480/80 = 6	-80	-80 - 20 = -100 B is 20 km/h faster than A. - sign only mentions the direction of the velocity. For magnitude, we need to add -20.	480/100 = 4.8	6 - 4.8 = 1.2 **This should be 2!**
480/60 = 8	60	60 + 20 = 80	480/80 = 6	8 - 6 = 2 **This is correct !**

So, VA = 60 km/h is the only answer satisfying the question.

25. A
First, insert the values of x and y into the expression given:
(x + y) / (x - y) = (√7 - 1 + √7 + 1) / (√7 - 1 - (√7 + 1))

= (2√7) / (√7 - 1 - √7 - 1) = (2√7) / (- 2) = - √7

26. A
-x - 7 = -3x - 9
-x + 3x = -9 + 7
2x = -2
x = (-2):2
x = -1

27. D
This is an inverse ratio problem. There are 6 workers in the beginning. Assume that each worker completes x work per day. Then, 6 workers will complete 6x work per day. On the second day, one worker leaves; so 5x work will be completed. The next day 4x and eventually 3x work will be completed on the 4th day. Since the job is completed in 4 days; 6x + 5x + 4x + 3x = 18x is the total work done. If no one leaves the work; there will be 6x work completed per day. As we know,

the total work is 18x, so,

18x / 6x = 3 days, so 6 workers would complete the construction of the wall.

28. B

First, notice that the numbers within the roots are not prime numbers, so we need to search for perfect squares to take out of the root and prepare for the possibility to simplify:

($\sqrt{75}$ - 3$\sqrt{48}$) / $\sqrt{147}$ + 20 = ($\sqrt{(3.25)}$ - 3$\sqrt{(3.16)}$) / $\sqrt{(3.49)}$ + $\sqrt{(5.4)}$

= ($\sqrt{(3.5^2)}$ - 3$\sqrt{(3.4^2)}$) / $\sqrt{(3.7^2)}$ + $\sqrt{(5.2^2)}$

= (5$\sqrt{3}$ - 12$\sqrt{3}$) / 7$\sqrt{3}$ + 2$\sqrt{5}$

= (- 7$\sqrt{3}$) / 7$\sqrt{3}$ + 2$\sqrt{5}$ = - 1 + 2$\sqrt{5}$

Now, we need to find the approximate value of $\sqrt{5}$ to tenths digit. To find the square root of 5 manually, we need to separate the number with all decimals in pairs starting from right. First, we search for the highest square smaller than 5. That is 4 and its square root is 2. In the upper part, we write this as the integer part of the square root of 5, then subtract 4 from 5. We obtain 1, then we write down double zero next to it. On the left hand side, we multiply 2 by 2 and obtain 4. Now, we search for a number to write next to 4 that will make the highest number smaller than 100 when multiplied by itself. We notice that 42 times 2 is 84 that is the highest. (43 times 3 exceeds 100) We write number "2" next to the integer part 2, after decimal point. Then, we subtract 84 from 100 and obtain 1600 by adding double zero next to the difference. On the left side; we multiply number "2" in 42 by 2 and obtain 4. Since this is smaller than 10, we directly write 4 in 42 in front of the 4 obtained by multiplication. Now, we search for a number to write next to 44 that will make the highest number smaller than 1600 when multiplied by itself. That is 3. We write this next to 2.2 and we continue so on. This operation can be continued infinitely.

```
              2.236...
  2       √5.00 00 00 ....
             - 4
 42         1 00
            - 84
```

44<u>3</u>   16 00
           - 1329
449<u>6</u>   271 00
           - 26976
                124

$\sqrt{5}$ = 2.236... continues. We need to round this result to tenths digit; that is 2.2.

So, the result - 1 + 2$\sqrt{5}$ is approximated to -1 + 2 * 22 = -1 + 4.4 = 3.4

29. D
In this type of question with one root within the other, we need to reduce the expression to one root with one degree that is found by multiplying all degrees of roots that follow each other.

Meanwhile; while taking a number inside a root, we need to take its power that is the degree of the root:

$^4\sqrt{(2 * \,^3\sqrt{4})} * \,^3\sqrt{\sqrt{8}} = \,^6\sqrt{(4 * \,^2\sqrt{2^{x+1}})}$
= $^{4.3}\sqrt{(2^3 * 4)} * \,^{3.2}\sqrt{8} = \,^{6.2}\sqrt{(4^2 * 2^{x+1})}$

Notice that every term is a power of 2, so write all of them in base 2:
= $^{12}\sqrt{(2^3 * 2^2)} * \,^6\sqrt{2^3} = \,^{12}\sqrt{(2^4 * 2^{x+1})}$
= $^{12}\sqrt{2^5} * \,^6\sqrt{2^3} = \,^{12}\sqrt{2^{x+5}}$
= $2^{5/12} * 2^{3/6} = 2^{(x+5)/12}$
= $2^{(5/12 + 1/2)} = 2^{(x+5)/12}$

Now that the bases are the same, we can equate the powers:

5/12 + 1/2 = (x + 5) / 12
(5 + 6) / 12 = (x + 5) / 12
11 = x + 5
x = 6

30. A
((1 - 1/3) * (1 + 1/5)) / (1/8 * 4/5 - 1/3)
First, we need to do the operations inside parenthesis and the multiplications. In the nominator, we need to do one subtraction and one addition operation:

= ((3/3 - 1/3) * (5/5 + 1/5)) / (4 / (8 * 5) - 1/3)

Now, we can subtract and add the fractions having the same denominators. Also, in the denominator; numbers 4 and 8 can be simplified by 4:

= (2/3 * 6/5) / (1/10 - 1/3)

Here, 3 and 6 are simplified by 3; meanwhile, the subtraction operation in the denominator is performed by the use of lcm (least common multiplier) that is 30 for 3 and 10:

= (4/5) / (3/30 - 10/30)
= (4/5) / ((3 - 10) / 30)
= (4/5) / (-7/30)

Now, we have two fractions that are divided. We can turn this operation into multiplication by simply changing the values of the denominator and the numerator of the second fraction as below:

= (4/5) * (-30/7)

Note that we use parenthesis since the second fraction is negative. We can also write the minus sign in the front of the expression. Now, we can simplify 30 and 5 by 5:
= -(4 * 6) / 7 = -24/7

= $(1/2)a^{-2}b^{3}c^{-11}$

Practice Test Questions Set 2

The questions below are not the same as you will find on the BC Police - that would be too easy! And nobody knows what the questions will be and they change all the time. Below are general questions that cover the same subject areas as the BC Police. So the format and exact wording of the questions may differ slightly, and change from year to year, if you can answer the questions below, you will have no problem with the BC Police.

For the best results, take these Practice Test Questions as if it were the real exam. Set aside time when you will not be disturbed, and a location that is quiet and free of distractions. Read the instructions carefully, read each question carefully, and answer to the best of your ability.
Use the bubble answer sheets provided. When you have completed the Practice Questions, check your answer against the Answer Key and read the explanation provided.

Do not attempt more than one set of practice test questions in one day. After completing the first practice test, wait two or three days before attempting the second set of questions.

Reading Comprehension

	A	B	C	D	E		A	B	C	D	E
1	○	○	○	○	○	21	○	○	○	○	○
2	○	○	○	○	○	22	○	○	○	○	○
3	○	○	○	○	○	23	○	○	○	○	○
4	○	○	○	○	○	24	○	○	○	○	○
5	○	○	○	○	○	25	○	○	○	○	○
6	○	○	○	○	○	26	○	○	○	○	○
7	○	○	○	○	○	27	○	○	○	○	○
8	○	○	○	○	○	28	○	○	○	○	○
9	○	○	○	○	○	29	○	○	○	○	○
10	○	○	○	○	○	30	○	○	○	○	○
11	○	○	○	○	○						
12	○	○	○	○	○						
13	○	○	○	○	○						
14	○	○	○	○	○						
15	○	○	○	○	○						
16	○	○	○	○	○						
17	○	○	○	○	○						
18	○	○	○	○	○						
19	○	○	○	○	○						
20	○	○	○	○	○						

Memory

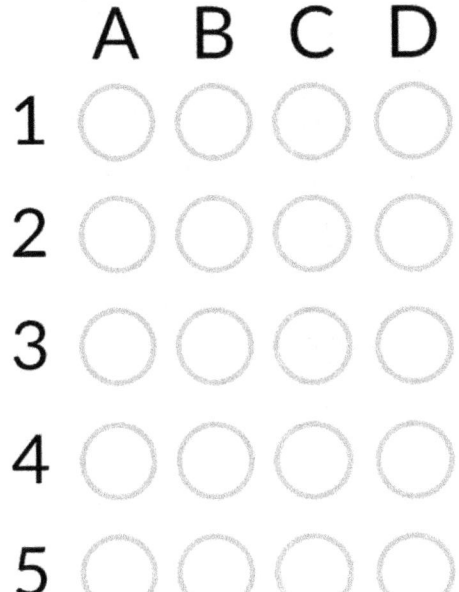

ENGLISH

	A	B	C	D	E			A	B	C	D	E
1	○	○	○	○	○		21	○	○	○	○	○
2	○	○	○	○	○		22	○	○	○	○	○
3	○	○	○	○	○		23	○	○	○	○	○
4	○	○	○	○	○		24	○	○	○	○	○
5	○	○	○	○	○		25	○	○	○	○	○
6	○	○	○	○	○		26	○	○	○	○	○
7	○	○	○	○	○		27	○	○	○	○	○
8	○	○	○	○	○		28	○	○	○	○	○
9	○	○	○	○	○		29	○	○	○	○	○
10	○	○	○	○	○		30	○	○	○	○	○
11	○	○	○	○	○							
12	○	○	○	○	○							
13	○	○	○	○	○							
14	○	○	○	○	○							
15	○	○	○	○	○							
16	○	○	○	○	○							
17	○	○	○	○	○							
18	○	○	○	○	○							
19	○	○	○	○	○							
20	○	○	○	○	○							

Math

	A	B	C	D	E			A	B	C	D	E
1	○	○	○	○	○		21	○	○	○	○	○
2	○	○	○	○	○		22	○	○	○	○	○
3	○	○	○	○	○		23	○	○	○	○	○
4	○	○	○	○	○		24	○	○	○	○	○
5	○	○	○	○	○		25	○	○	○	○	○
6	○	○	○	○	○		26	○	○	○	○	○
7	○	○	○	○	○		27	○	○	○	○	○
8	○	○	○	○	○		28	○	○	○	○	○
9	○	○	○	○	○		29	○	○	○	○	○
10	○	○	○	○	○		30	○	○	○	○	○
11	○	○	○	○	○							
12	○	○	○	○	○							
13	○	○	○	○	○							
14	○	○	○	○	○							
15	○	○	○	○	○							
16	○	○	○	○	○							
17	○	○	○	○	○							
18	○	○	○	○	○							
19	○	○	○	○	○							
20	○	○	○	○	○							

Reading Comprehension

Questions 1 - 4 refer to the following passage.

Passage 1 - The Crusades

In 1095 Pope Urban II proclaimed the First Crusade with the intent and stated goal to restore Christian access to holy places in and around Jerusalem. Over the next 200 years there were 6 major crusades and numerous minor crusades in the fight for control of the "Holy Land." Historians are divided on the real purpose of the Crusades, some believing that it was part of a purely defensive war against Islamic conquest; some see them as part of a long-running conflict at the frontiers of Europe; and others see them as confident, aggressive, papal-led expansion attempts by Western Christendom. The impact of the crusades was profound, and judgment of the Crusaders ranges from laudatory to highly critical. However, all agree that the Crusades and wars waged during those crusades were brutal and often bloody. Several hundred thousand Roman Catholic Christians joined the Crusades, they were Christians from all over Europe.

Europe at the time was under the Feudal System, so, while the Crusaders made vows to the Church, they also were beholden to their Feudal Lords. This led to the Crusaders not only fighting the Saracen, the commonly used word for Muslim at the time, but also each other for power and economic gain in the Holy Land. This infighting between the Crusaders is why many historians hold the view that the Crusades were simply a front for Europe to invade the Holy Land for economic gain in the name of the Church. Another factor contributing to this theory is that while the army of crusaders marched towards Jerusalem they pillaged the land as they went. The church and feudal Lords vowing to return the land to its original beauty, and inhabitants, this rarely happened though, as the Lords often kept the land for themselves. A full 800 years after the Crusades, Pope John Paul II expressed his sorrow for the massacre of innocent people and the lasting damage that the Medieval church caused.

1. What is the tone of this article?

    a. Subjective

    b. Objective

    c. Persuasive

    d. None of the Above

2. What can all historians agree on concerning the Crusades?

    a. It achieved great things

    b. It stabilized the Holy Land

    c. It was bloody and brutal

    d. It helped defend Europe from the Byzantine Empire

3. What impact did the feudal system have on the Crusades?

    a. It unified the Crusaders

    b. It helped gather volunteers

    c. It had no effect on the Crusades

    d. It led to infighting, causing more damage than good

4. What does Saracen mean?

    a. Muslim

    b. Christian

    c. Knight

    d. Holy Land

Questions 5 - 8 refer to the following passage.

ABC Electric Warranty

ABC Electric Company warrants that its products are free from defects in material and workmanship. Subject to the conditions and limitations set forth below, ABC Electric will, at its option, either repair or replace any part of its products that prove defective due to improper workmanship or materials.

This limited warranty does not cover any damage to the product from improper installation, accident, abuse, misuse, natural disaster, insufficient or excessive electrical supply, abnormal mechanical or environmental conditions, or any unauthorized disassembly, repair, or modification.

This limited warranty also does not apply to any product on which the original identification information has been altered, or removed, has not been handled or packaged correctly, or has been sold as second-hand.

This limited warranty covers only repair, replacement, refund or credit for defective ABC Electric products, as provided above.

5. I tried to repair my ABC Electric blender, but could not, so can I get it repaired under this warranty?

    a. Yes, the warranty still covers the blender

    b. No, the warranty does not cover the blender

    c. Uncertain. ABC Electric may or may not cover repairs under this warranty

6. My ABC Electric fan is not working. Will ABC Electric provide a new one or repair this one?

    a. ABC Electric will repair my fan

    b. ABC Electric will replace my fan

    c. ABC Electric could either replace or repair my fan can request either a replacement or a repair.

7. My stove was damaged in a flood. Does this warranty cover my stove?

    a. Yes, it is covered.

    b. No, it is not covered.

    c. It may or may not be covered.

    d. ABC Electric will decide if it is covered

8. Which of the following is an example of improper workmanship?

    a. Missing parts

    b. Defective parts

    c. Scratches on the front

    d. None of the above

Questions 9 – 12 refer to the following passage.

Passage 2 - Women and Advertising

Only in the last few generations have media messages been so widespread and so readily seen, heard, and read by so many people. Advertising is an important part of both selling and buying anything from soap to cereal to jeans. For whatever reason, more consumers are women than are men. Media message are subtle but powerful, and more attention has been paid lately to how these message affect women.

Of all the products that women buy, makeup, clothes, and other stylistic or cosmetic products are among the most popular. This means that companies focus their advertising on women, promising them that their product will make her feel, look, or smell better than the next company's product will. This competition has resulted in advertising that is more and more ideal and less and less possible for everyday women. However, because women do look to these ideals and the products they represent as how they can potentially become, many women have developed unhealthy attitudes about themselves when they have failed to become those ideals.

In recent years, more companies have tried to change advertisements to be healthier for women. This includes featuring models of more sizes and addressing a huge outcry against unfair tools such as airbrushing and photo editing. There is debate about what the right balance between real and ideal is, because fashion is also considered art and some changes are made to elevate fashionable products purposefully and signify that they are creative, innovative, and the work of individual people. Artists want their freedom protected as much as women do, and advertising agencies are often caught in the middle.

Some claim that the companies who make these changes are not doing enough. Many people worry that there are still not enough models of different sizes and different ethnicities.

Some people claim that companies use this healthier type of advertisement not for the good of women, but because they would like to sell products to the women who are looking for these kinds of messages. This is also a hard balance to find: companies need to make money, and women need to feel respected.

While the focus of this change has been on women, advertising can also affect men, and this change will hopefully be a lesson on media for all consumers.

9. The second paragraph states that advertising focuses on women

    a. to shape what the ideal should be

    b. because women buy makeup

    c. because women are easily persuaded

    d. because of the types of products that women buy

10. According to the passage, fashion artists and female consumers are at odds because

    a. there is a debate going on and disagreement drives people apart

    b. both of them are trying to protect their freedom to do something

    c. artists want to elevate their products above the reach of women

    d. women are creative, innovative, individual people

11. The author uses the phrase "for whatever reason" in this passage to

    a. keep the focus of the paragraph on media messages and not on the differences between men and women

    b. show that the reason for this is unimportant

    c. argue that it is stupid that more women are consumers than men

    d. show that he or she is tired of talking about why media messages are important

12. This passage suggests that

    a. advertising companies are still working on making their messages better

    b. all advertising companies seek to be more approachable for women

    c. women are only buying from companies that respect them

    d. artists could stop producing fashionable products if they feel bullied

Questions 13 - 16 refer to the following passage.

FDR, the Treaty of Versailles, and the Fourteen Points

At the conclusion of World War I, those who had won the war and those who were forced to admit defeat welcomed the end of the war and expected that a peace treaty would be signed. The American president, Franklin D. Roosevelt, played an important part in proposing what the agreements should be and did so through his Fourteen Points.
World War I had begun in 1914 when an Austrian archduke was assassinated, leading to a domino effect that pulled the world's most powerful countries into war on a large scale. The war catalysed the creation and use of deadly weapons that had not previously existed, resulting in a great loss of soldiers on both sides of the fighting. More than 9 million soldiers were killed.

The United States agreed to enter the war right before it ended, and many believed that its decision to become finally involved brought on the end of the war. FDR made it very clear that the U.S. was entering the war for moral reasons and had an agenda focused on world peace. The Fourteen Points were individual goals and ideas (focused on peace, free trade, open communication, and self-reliance) that FDR wanted the power nations to strive for now that the war had ended. He was optimistic and had many ideas about what could be accomplished through, and during the post-war peace. However, FDR's fourteen points were poorly received when he presented them to the leaders of other world powers, many of whom wanted only to help their own countries and to punish the Germans for fueling the war, and they fell by the wayside. World War II was imminent, for Germany lost everything.

Some historians believe that the other leaders who participated in the Treaty of Versailles weren't receptive to the Fourteen Points because World War I was fought almost entirely on European soil, and the United States lost much less than did the other powers. FDR was in a unique position to determine the fate of the war, but doing it on his own terms did not help accomplish his goals. This is only one historical example of how the United State has tried to use its power as an important country, but found itself limited because of geological or ideological factors.

13. The main idea of this passage is that

    a. World War I was unfair because no fighting took place in America

    b. World War II happened because of the Treaty of Versailles

    c. the power the United States has to help other countries also prevents it from helping other countries

    d. Franklin D. Roosevelt was one of the United States' smartest presidents

14. According to the second paragraph, World War I started because

    a. an archduke was assassinated

    b. weapons that were more deadly had been developed

    c. a domino effect of allies agreeing to help one another

    d. the world's most powerful countries were large

15. The author includes the detail that 9 million soldiers were killed

    a. to demonstrate why European leaders were hesitant to accept peace

    b. to show the reader the dangers of deadly weapons

    c. to make the reader think about which countries lost the most soldiers

    d. to demonstrate why World War II was imminent

16. According to this passage, catalysed means

    a. analyzed

    b. sped up

    c. invented

    d. funded

Questions 17 - 21 refer to the following passage.

Work-Life Balance

There is a worldwide pursuit for work-life balance. Work-life balance is not the equal division of time for both work and life. It would be unrealistic and unrewarding to schedule equal number of hours for both. Life activities should be ranked over work sometimes. The concept of work-life balance supports that employees should split their time, effort and energies for important aspects of their life and work.

Work-life balance varies over time depending on the daily requirements of personal life and workplace. A balance which best suits today can be different tomorrow. It is a daily effort to give time to family, friends, spirituality, self-care and personal growth along with demands of work. This balance also varies from person to person as all have different priorities and different life setups. A balance for a single individual is different to a married one. A quest for work-life balance reduces the stress in employees. Employers can help employees achieve work-life balance by offering them opportunities like: pay-time off policies, flexible work schedules. By doing this, a work environment is created where employees are mentally relaxed, perform outstandingly and growth outcomes are productive.
Core of an effective work-life balance is linked with 'Enjoyment' and 'Achievement.' Both enjoyment and Achievement are linked together like front and back of a coin in life. They come together in life; as you can't have a coin with single side. When one tries to live a one-sided life, it ends in the parade of successful people who are not 'happy' with their lives. Focusing on enjoyment and achievement everyday will help one reach that balance. The concept is to aim for achieving something 'today' and enjoying 'today' to have a good day. By doing it every day, soon one will have a pretty good 'life.' Daily achievement and enjoyment' has four quadrants; by focusing on these, overall work-life balance can be attained. These are: Work, Family, Friends and Self. If one can strive to enjoy and achieve all these four aspects 'every day', work-life balance is maintained. Employers as well as employees can gain equal benefit by offering work-

life balance choice s. Poor work-life balance is regressing for both employees and employers. It leads to stressed, absent employee and overall low output. Research shows that work-life 'imbalance' is linked with heart diseases, weak immune system, migraines, headache, back ache, stiff muscles, acne, depression, nervousness, lack of focus & concentration, forgetfulness, irritability, fatigue, insecurities and lower self-esteem. One needs to take control of his career, schedule and personal life and struggle to achieve a work-life balance for overall wellbeing.

17. Which of the following best describes "Work-life balance" according to the author?

   a. Work-life balance refers to prioritizing ones' personal life over professional life.

   b. Work-life balance is the necessary division of 24 hours of the day into work & personal life.

   c. Work-life balance is the art of prioritizing important traits of work and life without compromising either.

   d. Work-life balance is the ability to fail and yet be consistent at the same time.

18. Which of the following statements is TRUE according to the passage?

   a. Unmarried employees usually achieve better work-life balance as compared to married people.

   b. Work-life balance should remain static throughout the career of a person.

   c. One should strive to achieve 'today' and enjoy later after turning into a successful person.

   d. None of the above

19. which of the following factors is involved in the quadrant suggested for Daily achievement and enjoyment.

   a. Pets
   b. Friends
   c. Team
   d. Boss

20. According to the author, which of the following best describe the attributes linked with effective work-life balance?

   a. Desire and satisfaction
   b. Accomplishment and pleasure
   c. Success and Fortune
   d. Failure and Motivation

21. What are the possible benefits of maintaining work-life balance?

   a. Various physiological and psychological disorders can be avoided.
   b. One can become a successful person who is happy with his life.
   c. One can manage to meet the demands of professional, social and personal life.
   d. All of the above.

Questions 22 - 26 refer to the following passage.

Paleolithic diet

Our present genomic composition is a result of series of evolutionary events that taken place since the beginning of human life on this planet. Our current human form has undergone multiple genetic modifications; these evolutionary events have taken place in a special environment which is called the 'evolutionary environment of adaptation (EEA). This environment is not at a specific place or time, but rather an environment where a species evolves. For example, humans of one era evolve to adapt to the changes in environment; this helps their survival in the future environment. Different hypothesis explain that in the past, environmental changes have been so rapid that a disjunction has appeared between the previous and the present environment. Due to this rapid change, our genetics did not have enough time to adapt. This inadequate genetic adaptation has resulted in diseases, which s are regarded as 'disease of civilization.' Diseases which are common now were unknown to our ancestors.

There is an important link between food and disease. Food revolution and industrialization has had a significant impact on our diet. There is a huge difference between modern and Paleolithic diet. Paleolithic diet is the diet of our hunter-gatherer ancestors. Paleolithic humans started to grow plants and domesticate animals for food. Their diet consisted mainly of nuts, fruits, meat (land and sea animals) and some insects. It lacked processed food. If a food pyramid for Paleolithic diet is created (from top to bottom), it will include: carbohydrates, fats, whole wheat/grains, dairy, fish, lean meat, vegetables and fruits. Over time, changes in our diet have been faster than our physiological and metabolic adaptation can accommodate. This mismatch has lead to multiple health problems like obesity, heart diseases, diabetes, colon cancers, lungs diseases and dental problems.

Our ancestors had low blood pressure i.e. they were not hypertensive like many today. They had less body fat, better eye sight, stronger bones, fewer fractures and better insulin tolerance than most people today. They didn't die of diseases of civilization. Multiple studies show that by adopting a Paleolithic diet, our health improves dramatically. Patients of diabetes and heart diseases showed big improvement by following Paleolithic diet plans. Many people are trying to follow Paleolithic diet plans to lose weight or maintain healthy body weight. Paleolithic diet is known to best suit our genetics and hence, our bodies function optimally.

22. Which of the following CANNOT be inferred directly from the passage?

   a. Survival of humans depends on their ability to adapt to environmental changes and undergo the required genetic modifications.

   b. Hypertension is one diseases of civilization.

   c. Our ancestors enjoyed better health conditions since the environmental changes were slower at their time.

   d. Use of Paleolithic diet helps one to enjoy better health and avoid numerous diseases.

23. Which of the following cause(s) are linked with 'diseases of civilization' according to the passage?

   a. Inadequate genetic adaptation

   b. Smog in the modern environment

   c. Rapid pace of environmental changes

   d. Both A and C

24. Which of the following best explains the discordance hypothesis?

   a. Quality of diet of a person is directly proportional to his health.

   b. Environmental changes caused genetic incoherence leading to various diseases.

   c. Environmental evolution of a society is dependent on its biological evolution.

   d. Diseases of modern civilization have been inherited through the genes of our ancestors.

25. According to the passage, which of the following is NOT correct about Paleolithic diet?

   a. Paleolithic diet is a result of food revolution

   b. Paleolithic diet adopted by our ancestors included fats

   c. Cardiovascular diseases can be controlled by following Paleolithic diet

   d. Paleolithic diet suits our genes naturally

26. Which of the following would represent 'modern diet' as referred in the passage?

   a. Sea animals
   b. Nuts
   c. Bread
   d. Dairy

Questions 27 - 29 refer to the following passage.

Lowest Price Guarantee

Get it for less. Guaranteed!

ABC Electric will beat any advertised price by 10% of the difference.

   1) If you find a lower advertised price, we will beat it by 10% of the difference.

   2) If you find a lower advertised price within 30 days* of your purchase we will beat it by 10% of the difference.

   3) If our own price is reduced within 30 days* of your purchase, bring in your receipt and we will refund the difference.

*14 days for computers, monitors, printers, laptops, tablets, cellular & wireless devices, home security products, projectors, camcorders, digital cameras, radar detectors, portable DVD players, DJ and pro-audio equipment, and air conditioners.

27. I bought a radar detector 15 days ago and saw an ad for the same model only cheaper. Can I get 10% of the difference refunded?

    a. Yes. Since it is less than 30 days, you can get 10% of the difference refunded.

    b. No. Since it is more than 14 days, you cannot get 10% of the difference re-funded.

    c. It depends on the cashier.

    d. Yes. You can get the difference refunded.

28. I bought a flat-screen TV for $500 10 days ago and found an advertisement for the same TV, at another store, on sale for $400. How much will ABC refund under this guarantee?

    a. $100

    b. $110

    c. $10

    d. $400

29. What is the purpose of this passage?

    a. To inform

    b. To educate

    c. To persuade

    d. To entertain

Questions 30 refers to the following passage.

Passage 6 - What Is Mardi Gras?

Mardi Gras is fast becoming one of the South's most famous and most celebrated holidays. The word Mardi Gras comes from the French and the literal translation is "Fat Tuesday." The holiday has also been called Shrove Tuesday, due to its associations with Lent. The purpose of Mardi Gras is to celebrate and enjoy before the Lenten season of fasting and repentance begins.

What originated by the French Explorers in New Orleans, Louisiana in the 17th century is now celebrated all over the world. Panama, Italy, Belgium and Brazil all host large scale Mardi Gras celebrations, and many smaller cities and towns celebrate this fun loving Tuesday as well. Usually held in February or early March, Mardi Gras is a day of extravagance, a day for people to eat, drink and be merry, to wear costumes, masks and to dance to jazz music.
The French explorers on the Mississippi River would be in shock today if they saw the opulence of the parades and floats that grace the New Orleans streets during Mardi Gras these days. Parades in New Orleans are divided by organizations. These are more commonly known as Krewes.

Being a member of a Krewe is quite a task because Krewes are responsible for overseeing the parades. Each Krewe's parade is ruled by a Mardi Gras "King and Queen." The role of the King and Queen is to "bestow" gifts on their adoring fans as the floats ride along the street. They throw doubloons, which is fake money and usually colored green, purple and gold, which are the colors of Mardi Gras. Beads in those color shades are also thrown and cups are thrown as well. Beads are by far the most popular souvenir of any Mardi Gras parade, with each spectator attempting to gather as many as possible.

30. The purpose of Mardi Gras is to

    a. Repent for a month.

    b. Celebrate in extravagant ways.

    c. Be a member of a Krewe.

    d. Explore the Mississippi.

Memory

Directions: You have five minutes to memorize the following information. Do not write anything down. Questions follow on page 228.

Name: Janet Benoit
Description: Caucasian female with shoulder length hair. Heart tattoo on right arm.

Wanted for: Child neglect

Name: Robby Valence

Description: 5 ft 5 in Caucasian male, stocky build, no identifying marks

Wanted for: Armed Robbery

Make and Model: Volkswagen Passat

License: British Columbia MN1 23C

Wanted in Connection with: Dangerous Driving

Make and Model: Volkswagen Phaeton

License: Ontario MUYR-123

Wanted in Connection with: Fraud

Name: Nathan Abraham

Description: Black Canadian Male, 5 ft 1 in. no identifying features

Wanted for: Domestic Assault

Name: Jeffrey Crisp

Description: 5 ft 6 in Caucasian male, slight build, no identifying marks

Wanted for: Sexual Assault

Make and Model: Modified Honda Accord

License: Quebec A12 BRP

Wanted for: Homicide

Make and Model: Modified Chevrolet Truck

License: Yukon RTJ12

Wanted in Connection with: Uttering Threats

Memory

Questions 1 - 5 refer to the information above.

1. Who is wanted for child neglect?

    a. Robby Valence
    b. Janet Benoit
    c. Jeffrey Crisp
    d. Nathan Abraham

2. Who is wanted for sexual assault?

    a. Robby Valence
    b. Janet Benoit
    c. Jeffrey Crisp
    d. Nathan Abraham

3. What province is the Volkswagen Phaeton from?

    a. Yukon
    b. Quebec
    c. Ontario
    c. British Columbia

4. What is Nathan Abraham wanted for?

    a. Sexual Assault
    b. Armed Robbery
    c. Child Neglect
    d. Domestic Assault

5. What province is the modified Chevrolet truck from?

   a. Yukon

   b. Quebec

   c. Ontario

   c. British Columbia

ENGLISH

1. Choose the best definition of anecdote.

   a. A short account of an incident

   b. Something that comes before

   c. The use of humor, irony, exaggeration, or ridicule

   d. Constant fluctuations

2. Choose the adjective that means shocking, terrible or wicked.

   a. Pleasantries

   b. Heinous

   c. Shrewd

   d. Provincial

3. Choose the noun that means a person or thing that tells or announces the coming of someone or something.

   a. Harbinger

   b. Evasion

   c. Bleak

   d. Craven

4. Choose a word that means the same as the underlined word.

He wasn't especially generous. All the servings were very judicious.

    a. Abundant
    b. Careful
    c. Extravagant
    d. Careless

5. Fill in the blank.

Because of the growing use of _____ as a fuel, corn production has greatly increased.

    a. Alcohol
    b. Ethanol
    c. Natural gas
    d. Oil

6. Fill in the blank.

In heavily industrialized areas, the pollution of the air causes many to develop _____ diseases.

    a. Respiratory
    b. Cardiac
    c. Alimentary
    d. Circulatory

7. Choose the best definition of inherent.

    a. To receive money in a will
    b. An essential part of
    c. To receive money from a will
    d. None of the above

8. Choose the best definition of vapid.

   a. adj. tasteless or bland

   b. v. To inflict, as a revenge or punishment

   c. v. to convert into gas

   d. v. to go up in smoke

9. Choose the best definition of waif.

   a. n. a sick and hungry child

   b. n. an orphan staying in a foster home

   c. n. homeless child or stray

   d. n. a type of French bread eaten with cheese

10. Choose the adjective that means similar or identical.

   a. Soluble

   b. Assembly

   c. Conclave

   d. Homologous

11. Choose the correct spelling.

   a. Correspondence

   b. Corespodence

   c. Correspodence

   d. Correspomdence

12. Choose the correct spelling.

   a. Henmorrhage

   b. Hemmorrhage

   c. Hemorrhage

   d. Hemorhage

13. Choose the correct spelling.

    a. Enviromnment

    b. Environment

    c. Environiment

    d. Enviromment

14. Choose the correct spelling.

    a. Govermment

    b. Goverment

    c. Govenment

    d. Government

15. Choose the correct spelling.

    a. Conceeve

    b. Concieve

    c. Conceive

    d. Conceve

16. Choose the correct spelling.

    a. Describe

    b. Decribe

    c. Decsribe

    d. Discribe

17. Choose the correct spelling.

    a. Liqour

    b. Liquor

    c. Liquer

    d. Liquour

18. Choose the correct spelling.

    a. Succesful

    b. Sucessful

    c. Sucessfull

    d. Successful

19. Choose the correct spelling.

    a. Huricane

    b. Hurricane

    c. Huricane

    d. Hurriccane

20. Choose the correct spelling.

    a. Precede

    b. Preccede

    c. Precceed

    d. Preceed

21. Choose the sentence below with the correct punctuation.

    a. There are many species of owls, the Great-Horned Owl, the Snowy Owl, and the Western Screech Owl, and the Barn Owl.

    b. There are many species of owls, the Great-Horned Owl: the Snowy Owl: and the Western Screech Owl, and the Barn Owl.

    c. There are many species of owls: the Great-Horned Owl, the Snowy Owl, and the Western Screech Owl, and the Barn Owl.

    d. There are many species of owls: the Great-Horned Owl, the Snowy Owl, and the Western Screech Owl, and the Barn Owl.

22. Choose the sentence below with the correct punctuation.

a. In his most famous speech, Reverend King proclaimed: "I have a dream!"

b. In his most famous speech, Reverend King proclaimed; "I have a dream!"

c. In his most famous speech, Reverend King proclaimed. "I have a dream!"

d. In his most famous speech: Reverend King proclaimed, "I have a dream!"

23. Choose the sentence below with the correct punctuation.

a. Puzzled — Joe said, "You aren't going to pay me until ?"

b. Puzzled, Joe said, "You aren't going to pay me until ?"

c. Puzzled, Joe said, "You aren't going to pay me until —?"

d. Puzzled, Joe said, "You aren't going to pay me until, ?"

24. Choose the sentence with the correct usage.

a. Vegetables are a healthy food; eating them can make you more healthful.

b. Vegetables are a healthful food; eating them can make you more healthful.

c. Vegetables are a healthy food; eating them can make you more healthy.

d. Vegetables are a healthful food; eating them can make you more healthy.

25. Choose the sentence with the correct usage.

a. When James went into his room, he found that his clothes had been put in the closet.

b. When James went in his room, he found that his clothes had been put in the closet.

c. When James went into his room, he found that his clothes had been put into the closet.

d. When James went in his room, he found that his clothes had been put into the closet.

26. Choose the sentence with the correct usage.

a. After you lay the books on the counter, you may lay down for a nap.

b. After you lie the books on the counter, you may lay down for a nap.

c. After you lay the books on the counter, you may lie down for a nap.

d. After you lay the books on the counter, you may lay down for a nap.

27. Choose the sentence with the correct usage.

a. He did not have to loose the race; if only his shoes weren't so lose!

b. He did not have to lose the race; if only his shoes weren't so loose!

c. He did not have to loose the race; if only his shoes weren't so lose!

d. He did not have to lose the race; if only his shoes weren't so lose!

28. Choose the sentence with the correct usage.

a. The attorney did not want to prosecute the defendant; his goal was to prosecute the guilty party.

b. The attorney did not want to persecute the defendant; his goal was to persecute the guilty party.

c. The attorney did not want to prosecute the defendant; his goal was to persecute the guilty party.

d. The attorney did not want to persecute the defendant; his goal was to prosecute the guilty party.

29. Choose the sentence with the correct usage.

a. The speeches must precede the election; the election cannot proceed without hearing from the candidates.

b. The speeches must precede the election; the election cannot precede without hearing from the candidates.

c. The speeches must proceed the election; the election cannot precede without hearing from the candidates.

d. The speeches must proceed the election; the election cannot proceed without hearing from the candidates.

30. Choose the sentence with the correct usage.

a. Before a lawyer can rise an objection, he must first rise to his feet.

b. Before a lawyer can raise an objection, he must first raise to his feet.

c. Before a lawyer can raise an objection, he must first rise to his feet.

d. Before a lawyer can rise an objection, he must first raise to his feet.

MATH

1. Estimate 2009 x 108.

    a. 110,000

    b. 2,0000

    c. 21,000

    d. 210,000

2. Richard sold 12 shirts for total revenue of $336 at 8% profit. What is the purchase price of each shirt?

    a. $25.76

    b. $24.50

    c. $23.75

    d. $22.50

3. Calculate (3a + 4b) * d when A = 2, b = 4 and d = 8

    a. 40

    b. 150

    c. 112

    d. 176

4. c = 4, n = 5 and x = 3. Calculate 2cnx/2n

    a. 12

    b. 50

    c. 8

    d. 21

5. If a = 12 and b = 8, solve 6b - a + 2a

   a. 12/9
   b. 18
   c. 16
   d. 12

6. Solve √121

   a. 11
   b. 12
   c. 21
   d. None of the above

7. In a local election at polling station A, 945 voters cast their vote out of 1270 registered voters. At polling station B, 860 cast their vote out of 1050 registered voters and at station C, 1210 cast their vote out of 1440 registered voters. What was the total turnout including all three polling stations?

   a. 70%
   b. 74%
   c. 76%
   d. 80%

8. In a factory, the average salary of all employees is $125. The average salary of 10 managers is $300 and average salary of workers is $100. What is the total number of employees?

   a. 30
   b. 40
   c. 25
   d. 50

9. In a 30 minute test there are 40 problems. A student solved 28 problems in first 25 minutes. How many seconds should she give to each of the remaining problems?

    a. 20 seconds
    b. 23 seconds
    c. 25 seconds
    d. 27 seconds

10. The total expense of building a fence around a square-shaped field is $2000 at a rate of $5 per meter. What is the length of one side?

    a. 80 meters
    b. 100 meters
    c. 40 meters
    d. 320 meters

11. In a class of 83 students, 72 are present. What percent of student is absent? Provide answer up to two significant digits.

    a. 12
    b. 13
    c. 14
    d. 15

12. If Lynn can type a page in p minutes, what portion of the page can she do in 5 minutes?

    a. p/5
    b. p − 5
    c. p + 5
    d. 5/p

13. A worker's weekly salary was increased by 30%. If his new salary is $150, what was his old salary?

    a. $120.00
    b. $99.15
    c. $109.00
    d. $115.40

14. Brad has agreed to buy everyone a Coke. Each drink costs $1.89, and there are 5 friends. Estimate Brad's cost.

    a. $7
    b. $8
    c. $10
    d. $12

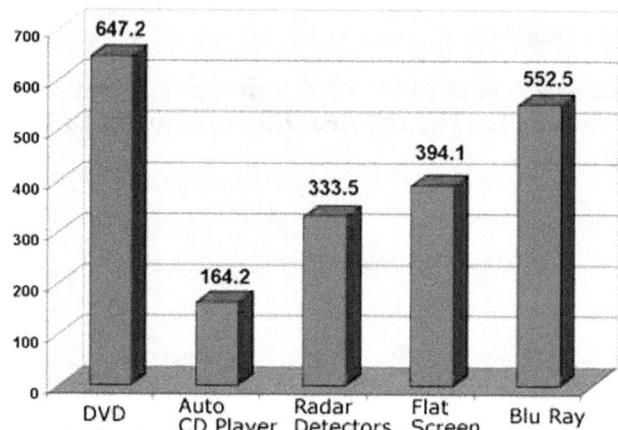

15. Consider the graph above. What is the third best-selling product?

    a. Radar Detectors
    b. Flat Screen TV
    c. Blu Ray
    d. Auto CD Players

16. Which two products are the closest in the number of sales?

    a. Blu Ray and Flat Screen TV
    b. Flat Screen TV and Radar Detectors
    c. Radar Detectors and Auto CD Players
    d. DVD players and Blu Ray

17. Great Britain has a Value Added Tax of 15%. A shop sells a camera for $545. If the VAT is included in the price, what is the actual cost of the camera?

    a. $490.40
    b. $473.91
    c. $505.00
    d. $503.15

18. The owner of a pet store decided to increase the cost of all reptiles 45%. If the initial cost of a reptile was $220, what is the new cost?

    a. $230
    b. $300
    c. $319
    d. $245

19. 5 men have to share a load weighing 10kg 550g equally among themselves. How much will each man have to carry?

    a. 900 g
    b. 1.5 kg
    c. 3 kg
    d. 2 kg 110 g

20. Peter drives 4 blocks to school and back every day. How many blocks does he drive in 5 days?

    a. 20
    b. 30
    c. 40
    d. 50

21. Simplify the following expression in rational number form:

$(\sqrt{4/9} * 3/8) / ((\sqrt[3]{125} / \sqrt[4]{81}) / 4 - 1/12)$.

    a. 1/2
    b. 3/4
    c. 4/3
    d. 2

22. What is the result of the expression $(i^{18} - i^5 + 4i^{162} - i^{39}) / (i^2 - 1)$?

    b. 2
    b. 5/2
    c. 7/2
    d. 5

23. Using the factoring method, solve the quadratic equation: $2x^2 - 3x = 0$

    a. 0 and 1.5
    b. 1.5 and 2
    c. 2 and 2.5
    d. 0 and 2

24. Using the quadratic formula, solve the quadratic equation: $x^2 - 9x + 14 = 0$

   a. 2 and 7
   b. -2 and 7
   c. -7 and -2
   d. -7 and 2

25. Factor the polynomial $9x^2 - 6x + 12$.

   a. $3(x^2 - 2x + 9)$
   b. $3(3x^2 - 3x + 4)$
   c. $9(x^2 - 3x + 3)$
   d. $3(3x^2 - 2x + 4)$

26. Factor the polynomial $x^3y^3 - x^2y^8$.

   a. $x^2y^3(x - y^5)$
   b. $x^3y^3(1 - y^5)$
   c. $x^2y^2(x - y^6)$
   d. $xy^3(x - y^5)$

27. $(3y^5 - 2y + y^4 + 2y^3 + 5) - (2y^5 + 3y^3 + 2 + 7y) =$

   a. $y^5 + y^4 - y^3 - 9y + 3$
   b. $y^5 + y^4 - y^3 - 7y + 2$
   c. $y^3 + y^4 - y^2 - 9y + 3$
   d. $y^2 + y^4 - 2y^3 - 3y + 3$

28. Add $-3x^2 + 2x + 6$ **and** $-x^2 - x - 1$.

   a. $-2x^2 + x + 5$
   b. $-4x^2 + x + 5$
   c. $-2x^2 + 3x + 5$
   d. $-4x^2 + 3x + 5$

29. Find x and y from the following system of equations:

(4x + 5y)/3 = ((x - 3y)/2) + 4
(3x + y)/2 = ((2x + 7y)/3) -1

    a. (1, 3)
    b. (2, 1)
    c. (1, 1)
    d. (0, 1)

30. The area of a rectangle is 20 cm². If one side increases by 1 cm and other by 2 cm, the area of the new rectangle is 35 cm². Find the sides of the original rectangle.

    a. (4,8)
    b. (4,5)
    c. (2.5,8)
    d. b and c

Answer Key

Reading Comprehension

1. A
Choice B is incorrect; the author did not express their opinion on the subject matter. Choice C is incorrect, the author was not trying to prove a point, nor is the author trying to persuade.

2. C
Choice C is correct; historians believe it was brutal and bloody. Choice A is incorrect; there is no consensus that the Crusades achieved great things. Choice B is incorrect; it did not stabilize the Holy Lands. Choice D is incorrect, some historians do believe this was the purpose but not all historians.

3. D
The feudal system led to infighting. Choice A is incorrect, it had the opposite effect. Choice B is incorrect, though this is a good answer, it is not the best answer. The Church asked for volunteers not the Feudal Lords. Choice C is incorrect, it did have an effect on the Crusades.

4. A
Saracen was a generic term for Muslims widely used in Europe during the later medieval era.

5. B
This warranty does not cover a product that you have tried to fix yourself. From paragraph two, "This limited warranty does not cover ... any unauthorized disassembly, repair, or modification. "

6. C
ABC Electric could either replace or repair the fan, provided the other conditions are met. ABC Electric has the option to repair or replace.

7. B

The warranty does not cover a stove damaged in a flood. From the passage, "This limited warranty does not cover any damage to the product from improper installation, accident, abuse, misuse, natural disaster, insufficient or excessive electrical supply, abnormal mechanical or environmental conditions."

A flood is an "abnormal environmental condition," and a natural disaster, so it is not covered.

8. A

A missing part is an example of defective workmanship. This is an error made in the manufacturing process. A defective part is not considered workmanship.

9. D

This question tests the reader's summarization skills. The other choices A, B, and C focus on portions of the second paragraph that are too narrow and do not relate to the specific portion of text in question. The complexity of the sentence may mislead students into selecting one of these answers, but rearranging or restating the sentence will lead the reader to the correct answer. In addition, choice A makes an assumption that may or may not be true about the intentions of the company, choice B focuses on one product rather than the idea of the products, and choice C makes an assumption about women that may or may not be true and is not supported by the text.

10. B

This question tests reader's attention to detail. If a reader selects A, he or she may have picked up on the use of the word "debate" and assumed, very logically, that the two are at odds because they are fighting; however, this is simply not supported in the text. Choice C also uses very specific quotes from the text, but it rearranges and gives them false meaning. The artists want to elevate their creations above the creations of other artists, thereby showing that they are "creative" and "innovative." Similarly, choice D takes phrases straight from the text and rearranges and confuses them. The artists are described as wanting to be "creative, innovative, individual people," not the women.

11. A

This question tests reader's vocabulary and summarization skills. This phrase, used by the author, may seem flippant and dismissive if readers focus on the word "whatever" and misinterpret it as a popular, colloquial term. In this way, choices B and C may mislead the reader to selecting one of them by including the terms "unimportant" and "stupid," respectively. Choice D is a similar misreading, but doesn't make sense when the phrase is at the beginning of the passage and the entire passage is on media messages. Choice A is literally and contextually appropriate, and the reader can understand that the author would like to keep the introduction focused on the topic the passage is going to discuss.

12. A

This question tests a reader's inference skills. The extreme use of the word "all" in choice B suggests that every single advertising company are working to be approachable, and while this is not only unlikely, the text specifically states that "more" companies have done this, signifying that they have not all participated, even if it's a possibility that they may some day. The use of the limiting word "only" in choice C lends that answer similar problems; women are still buying from companies who do not care about this message, or those companies would not be in business, and the passage specifies that "many" women are worried about media messages, but not all. Readers may find choice D logical, especially if they are looking to make an inference, and while this may be a possibility, the passage does not suggest or discuss this happening. Choice A is correct based on specifically because of the relation between "still working" in the answer and "will hopefully" and the extensive discussion on companies struggles, which come only with progress, in the text.

13. C

This question tests the reader's summarization skills. The entire passage is leading up to the idea that the president of the US may not have had grounds to assert his Fourteen Points when other countries had lost so much. Choice A is pretty directly inferred by the text, but it does not adequately summarize what the entire passage is trying to communicate. Choice B may also be inferred by the passage when it says that the war is "imminent," but it does not represent the entire message, either. The passage does seem to be in praise of FDR, or at least in respect of him, but it does not in any way claim that he is the smartest president, nor does this represent the many other points included. Choice C is then the obvious answer, and most directly relates to the closing sentences which it rewords.

14. C
This question tests the reader's attention to detail. The passage does state that choices A and B are true, and while those statements are in proximity to the explanation for why the war started, they are not the reason given. Choice D is a mix up of words used in the passage, which says that the largest powers were in play but not that this fact somehow started the war. The passage does make a direct statement that a domino effect started the war, supporting choice C as the correct answer.

15. A
This question tests the reader's understanding of functions in writing. Throughout the passage, it states that leaders of other nations were hesitant to accept generous or peaceful terms because of the grievances of the war, and the great loss of life was chief among these. While the passage does touch on the devastation of deadly weapons (B), the use of this raw, emotional fact serves a much larger purpose, and the focus of the passage is not the weapons. While readers may indeed consider who lost the most soldiers (C) when, so many countries were involved and the inequalities of loss are mentioned in the passage, there is no discussion of this in the passage. Choice D is related to A, but choice A is more direct and relates more to the passage.

16. B
This question tests the reader's vocabulary skills. Choice A may seem appealing to readers because it is phonetically similar to "catalysed," but the two are not related in any other way. Choice C makes sense in context, but if plugged in to the sentence creates a redundancy that doesn't make sense. Choice D does also not make sense contextually, even if the reader may consider that funds were needed to create more weaponry, especially if it was advanced.

17. C
Choice A is incorrect since work-life balance does not suggest a compromise with professional life. Choice B is discussed as incorrect in the passage. Choice D is also incorrect, and it has not been discussed in the passage. Choice C is the correct definition of work-life balance.

18. D
Choice A is incorrect because work-life balance varies with status. If maintained, unmarried and unmarried people can achieve it. Choice B is incorrect because work-life balance should keep shifting continuously according to priorities. Choice C is incorrect because one should try to achieve and enjoy at the same time.

19. B
Quadrant for daily achievement and enjoyment includes: Work, Self, Family and Friends. Choice B is correct.

20. B
According to the passage, two factors linked to effective work-life balance are "achievement" and "enjoyment". Choice B represents the best synonyms of these 2 factors. All other choices are incorrect.

21. D
Choices, A, B and C are discussed in the passage as advantages of maintaining work-life balance. Choice D is the correct answer.

22. B
Choice A is mentioned in the initial part of the passage, choices C and D are also discussed later in the passage. Choice B is the correct answer as it cannot be inferred from the passage, since the reason of better health conditions of ancestors has been the use of Paleolithic diet which helped them to adapt to environment and avoid diseases.

23. D
According to the passage, environmental changes has been rapid in the past, which did not allow humans to adapt accordingly, this resulted in disjunction between the present and past environment, and humans faced inadequate

genetic adaption. These factors led to diseases of civilization. Choices A and C are correct. Choice B is not discussed in the passage.

24. B
Choice A is not related to discordance hypothesis, although true. Choice B correctly explains the term where rapid environmental changes did not allow humans to adapt genetically and hence they developed diseases of civilization. Choices C and D are both erroneous facts and not true.

25. A
Choice A is incorrect since it's the opposite where revolution of food has lost the use of natural food. Paleolithic diet and processed food has become common. All other choices are true regarding Paleolithic diet as per the passage.

26. C
As per the passage, the modern diet usually includes processed food. In all the choices, only bread is a processed food which is the correct answer. All other choices are naturally produced.

27. B
The time limit for radar detectors is 14 days. Since you made the purchase 15 days ago, you do not qualify for the guarantee.

28. B
Since you made the purchase 10 days ago, you are covered by the guarantee. Since it is an advertised price at a different store, ABC Electric will "beat" the price by 10% of the difference, which is,

500 – 400 = 100 – difference in price

100 X 10% = $10 – 10% of the difference

The advertised lower price is $400. ABC will beat this price by 10% so they will refund $100 + 10 = $110.

29. C
The purpose of this passage is to persuade.

30. B
The correct answer can be found in the fourth sentence of the first paragraph.

Choice A is incorrect because repenting begins the day AFTER Mardi Gras. Choice C is incorrect because you can celebrate Mardi Gras without being a member of a Krewe.

Choice D is incorrect because exploration does not play any role in a modern Mardi Gras celebration.

Memory

1. B
Janet Benoit is wanted for child neglect.

2. C
Jeffrey Crisp is wanted for sexual assault.

3. C
The Volkswagen Phaeton is from Ontario.

4. D
Nathan Abraham is wanted for domestic assault.

5. A
The modified Chevrolet truck is from the Yukon.

English

1. A
Anecdote: n. A short account of an incident

2. B
Heinous: adj. shocking, terrible or wicked.

3. A
Harbinger: n. a person of thing that tells or announces the coming of someone or something

4. B
Judicious: Having, or characterized by, good judgment or sound thinking. Careful.

5. B
Ethanol: n. a colorless volatile flammable liquid C_2H_6O.

6. A
Respiratory: adj. Of, relating to, or affecting respiration or the organs of respiration.

7. B
Inherent: Naturally a part or consequence of something.

8. A
Vapid: adj. tasteless or bland.

9. C
Waif: n. homeless child or stray.

10. D
Homologous: adj. similar or identical.

11. A
Correspondence is the correct spelling.

12. C
Hemorrhage is the correct spelling.

13. B
Environment is the correct spelling.

14. D
Government is the correct spelling.

15. C
Conceive is the correct spelling.

16. A
Describe is the correct spelling.

17. B
Liquor is the correct spelling.

18. D
Successful is the correct spelling.

19. B
Hurricane is the correct spelling.

20. A
Precede is the correct spelling.

21. D
A colon informs the reader that what follows the mark proves, explains, or lists elements of what preceded the mark.

22. D
A colon informs the reader that what follows the mark proves, explains, or lists elements of what preceded the mark.

23. C
The dash is used when the speaker cannot continue.

24. D
Healthful vs. Healthy. Use 'Healthy' to describe something that is of good for your health and 'healthful' refers to habits or types.

25. A
In vs. Into. 'In' a room means inside. 'Into' refers to movement or action.

26. C
Lay vs. Lie. 'Lie' requires an object and 'lay' does not. So you can lie down, (no object. and you lay a book on the floor.

27. B
Lose vs. Loose. 'Lose' is to no longer have, or to lose a race. 'Loose' is not tied or able to move freely.

28. D
Persecute vs. Prosecute. To prosecute is to have a legal claim against someone and to persecute is to harass.

29. A
Precede vs. Proceed. To precede, is to go first or in front of. To proceed is to go forward.

30. C
Rise vs. Raise. 'Rise' does not require an object and raise does require an object. You have to 'raise' something.

MATH

1. D
2009 X 108 is about 210,000. The actual number is 216,972.

2. A
The price of 12 shirts with profit is 8% = 0.92 X 336 = $309.12 The purchase price of each shirt = 309.12/12 = $25.76

3. D
Substitute the known variables, (3 x 2) + (4 x 4) x 8 =, 6 + 16 x 8, 24 x 8 = 176

4. A
2cnx = 2(4 x 5 x 3)/(2 X 5) =, 2 x 60/2 x 5 =, 120/10 = 12

5. D
Substitute with known variables, (6 x 8) – 12 + (2 x 12) =, 48 – 12 + 24, do the additions first, 48 – (12 + 24) =, 48 – 36 = 12

6. A
$\sqrt{121}$ = 11

7. D
To find the total turnout in all three polling stations, we need to proportion the number of voters to the number of all registered voters.
Number of total voters = 945 + 860 + 1210 = 3015

Number of total registered voters
= 1270 + 1050 + 1440 = 3760
Percentage turnout over all three polling stations
= 3015 * 100/3760 = 80.19%

Checking the answers, we round 80.19 to the nearest whole number: 80%

8. B
Assume the total numbers of employees is x. The total salary of all employees will be 125x. The total salary of the managers = 10 X 300 = $3000. The number of employees = X - 10, so the total salary of employees will be 100 X (X-10). The equation becomes 100(X - 10) + 3000 = 125X. x = 40.

9. C
The number of remaining questions is 40 - 28 = 12
The time remaining is 30 - 25 = 5 minutes = 5 X 60 = 300 seconds. So the time remaining for each question is 300/12 = 25 seconds.

10. B
Total expense is $2000 and we are informed that $5 is spent per meter. Combining these two information, we know that the total length of the fence is 2000/5 = 400 meters.

The fence is built around a square-shaped field. If one side of the square is "a," the perimeter of the square is "4a." Here, the perimeter is equal to 400 meters. So,

400 = 4a

100 = a → this means that one side of the square is equal to 100 meters.

11. B
If 72 students are present, then 83 - 72 = 11 students are absent. To calculate the percent, the equation will be,

11/83 = x/100
83x = 1100
x = 1100/83
x = 13.25 rounding off - 13% of the students are absent.

12. D
This is a simple direct proportion problem:
If Lynn can type 1 page in p minutes, then she can type x pages in 5 minutes

Cross multiply: x * p = 5 * 1

Then,
x = 5/p

13. D
Let old salary = X, therefore $150 = x + 0.30x, 150 = 1x + 0.30x, 150 = 1.30x, x = 150/1.30 = 115.4

14. C
If there are 5 friends and each drink costs $1.89, we can round up to $2 per drink and estimate the total cost at, 5 X $2 = $10.

The actual, cost is 5 X $1.89 = $9.45.

15. B
Flat Screen TVs are the third best-selling product.

16. B
The two products that are closest in the number of sales, are Flat Screen TVs and Radar Detectors.

17. B
Actual cost = X, therefore, 545 = x + 0.15x, 545 = 1x + 0.15x, 545 = 1.15x, x = 545/1.15 = 473.91

18. C
Initial cost was $220. new cost = 220 + (45% of 220), 45% of 220, 45/100 x 220 = 99, therefore new price is 220 + 90 = $319

19. D
First convert the unit of measurements to be the same. Since 1000 g = 1 kg, 10 kg = 10 x 1000 = 10,000 + 550 g = 10,550 g. Divide 10,550 by 5 = 10550/5 = 2110 = 2 kg 110 g

20. C
Each round trip will be 8 blocks, so in 5 days, he will drive 5 X 8 = 40 blocks.

21. B

In this question, notice that there are different degrees of roots. When no number is mentioned as degree, it is square root. There are also 3rd and 4th degree of roots in this question. When taking the nth root of a number, we need to consider in the opposite direction. The nth root of the number is the number of which nth power is the number inside the root. So, $\sqrt{4/9} = \sqrt{4}/\sqrt{9} = 2/3$ since the square of 2 is 4 and the square of 3 is 9. Similarly; $\sqrt[3]{125} = \sqrt[3]{5^3} = 5$ and $\sqrt[4]{81} = \sqrt[4]{3^4} = 3$. Inserting these equivalences and doing the fractional operations, step by step solution is as follows:

$(\sqrt{4/9} * 3/8) / ((\sqrt[3]{125} / \sqrt[4]{81}) / 4 - 1/12) = (2/3 * 3/8) / (5/3 * 1/4 - 1/12)$
$= (1/4) / (5/12 - 1/12)$
$= (1/4) / ((5 - 1) / 12) = (1/4) / (4/12) = 1/4 * 12/4 = 3/4$

22. B

We know that $i^2 = -1$. However, in this question, we see high powers of i. We need to use modular arithmetic techniques to solve this problem:

$i^0 = 1$
$i^1 = i$
$i^2 = -1$
$i^3 = -i$
$i^4 = 1$
$i^5 = i$

This means that every 4 powers; we obtain i. So, by dividing the powers by 4; the remainder of the division operation will lead us to the result of powers:

$18/4 \rightarrow$ remainder = 2
$5/4 \rightarrow$ remainder = 1
$162/4 \rightarrow$ remainder = 2
$39/4 \rightarrow$ remainder = 3

Then;

$(i^{18} - i^5 + 4i^{162} - i^{39}) / (i^2 - 1) = (i^2 - i + 4*i^2 - i^3) / (-1 - 1)$
$= (-1 - i - 4*1 + i) / (-2)$
$= (-5) / (-2) = 5/2$

23. A
$2x^2 - 3x = 0$ ... we see that both of the terms contain x; so we can take it out as a factor:
$x(2x - 3) = 0$ ... two terms are multiplied and the result is zero. This means that either of the terms or, both can be equal to zero:

$x = 0$ ... this is one of the solutions

$2x - 3 = 0 \rightarrow 2x = 3 \rightarrow x = 3/2 \rightarrow x = 1.5$ ... this is the second solution.

So, the solutions are 0 and 1.5.

24. A
To solve the equation, we need the equation in the form $ax^2 + bx + c = 0$.

$x^2 - 9x + 14 = 0$ is already in this form.

The quadratic formula to find the roots of a quadratic equation is:

$x_{1,2} = (-b \pm \sqrt{\Delta}) / 2a$ where $\Delta = b^2 - 4ac$ and is called the discriminant of the quadratic equation.

In our question, the equation is $x^2 - 9x + 14 = 0$. By remembering the form $ax^2 + bx + c = 0$:

$a = 1, b = -9, c = 14$

So, we can find the discriminant first, and then the roots of the equation:

$\Delta = b^2 - 4ac = (-9)^2 - 4 * 1 * 14 = 81 - 56 = 25$

$x_{1,2} = (-b \pm \sqrt{\Delta}) / 2a = (-(-9) \pm \sqrt{25}) / 2 = (9 \pm 5) / 2$

This means that the roots are,

$x_1 = (9 - 5) / 2 = 2$ and $x_2 = (9 + 5) / 2 = 7$

25. D
$9x^2 - 6x + 12 = 3 * \underline{3}x^2 - 2 * \underline{3}x + \underline{3} * 4 = 3(3x^2 - 2x + 4)$

26. A
$x^3y^3 - x^2y^8 = x * \underline{x^2y^3} - \underline{x^2y^3} * y^5 = x^2y^3(x - y^5)$

27. A
Write in standard form $(3y^5 + y^4 + 2y^3 - 2y + 5) - (2y^5 + 3y^3 + 7y + 2)$
Arrange in columns of like terms and subtract bottom row

$3y^5 + y^4 + 2y^3 - 2y + 5$
$-2y^5 - 3y^3 - 7y - 2$

$y^5 + y^4 - y^3 - 9y + 3$

28. B
$(-3x^2 + 2x + 6) + (-x^2 - x - 1)$

$= -3x^2 + 2x + 6 - x^2 - x - 1$ ... we write similar terms together:

$= -3x^2 - x^2 + 2x - x + 6 - 1$ ... we operate within the same terms:

$= -4x^2 + x + 5$

29. C
First, we need to arrange the two equations to obtain the form $ax + by = c$. We see that there are 3 and 2 in the denominators of both equations. If we equate all at 6, then we can cancel all 6 in the denominators and have straight equations:

Equate all denominators at 6:

$2(4x + 5y)/6 = 3(x - 3y)/6 + 4 * 6/6$ ... Now we can cancel 6 in the denominators:

$8x + 10y = 3x - 9y + 24$ ... We can collect x and y terms on left side of the equation:

$8x + 10y - 3x + 9y = 24$

$5x + 19y = 24$ ... Equation (I)

Arrange the second equation:

$3(3x + y)/6 = 2(2x + 7y)/6 - 1 * 6/6$ ... Now we can cancel 6 in the denominators:

$9x + 3y = 4x + 14y - 6$ ... We can collect x and y terms on left side of the equation:

$9x + 3y - 4x - 14y = -6$

$5x - 11y = -6$ ... Equation (II)

Now, we have two equations and two unknowns x and y. By writing the two equations one under the other and operating, we can find one unknowns first, and find the other next:

$5x + 19y = 24$

$-1/\ 5x - 11y = -6$ ... If we substitute this equation from the upper one, 5x cancels -5x:

$5x + 19y = 24$

$-5x + 11y = 6$ ... Summing side-by-side:

$5x - 5x + 19y + 11y = 24 + 6$

$30y = 30$ ... Dividing both sides by 30:

$y = 1$

Inserting y = 1 into either of the equations, we can find the value of x. Choosing equation I:

$5x + 19 * 1 = 24$

$5x = 24 - 19$

$5x = 5$ ... Dividing both sides by 5:

$x = 1$

So, x = 1 and y = 1 is the solution; it is shown as (1, 1).

30. D
The area of a rectangle is found by multiplying the width to the length. If we call these sides with "a" and "b"; the area is = a * b.

We are given that a * b = 20 cm² ... Equation I

One side is increased by 1 and the other by 2 cm. So new side lengths are "a + 1" and "b + 2."

The new area is (a + 1)(b + 2) = 35 cm² ... Equation II

Using equations I and II, we can find a and b:

ab = 20

(a + 1)(b + 2) = 35 ... We need to distribute the terms in parenthesis:

ab + 2a + b + 2 = 35

We can insert ab = 20 to the above equation:

20 + 2a + b + 2 = 35

2a + b = 35 - 2 - 20

2a + b = 13 ... This is one equation with two unknowns. We need to use another information to have two equations with two unknowns which leads us to the solution. We know that ab = 20. So, we can use a = 20/b:

2(20/b) + b = 13

40/b + b = 13 ... We equate all denominators to "b" and eliminate it:

40 + b² = 13b

b² - 13b + 40 = 0 ... We can use the roots by factoring. We try to separate the middle term -13b to find common factors with b² and 40 separately:

b² - 8b - 5b + 40 = 0 ... Here, we see that b is a common factor for b² and -8b, and -5 is a common factor for -5b and 40:

b(b - 8) - 5(b - 8) = 0 Here, we have b times b - 8 and -5 times b - 8 summed up. This means that we have b - 5 times b - 8:

(b - 5)(b - 8) = 0

This is true when either, or both the expressions in the parenthesis are equal to zero:

b - 5 = 0 ... b = 5

b - 8 = 0 ... b = 8

So we have two values for b which means we have two values for 'a' as well. To find a, we can use any equation we have. Use a = 20/b.

If b = 5, a = 20/b → a = 4

If b = 8, a = 20/b → a = 2.5

So, (a, b) pairs for the sides of the original rectangle are: (4, 5) and (2.5, 8). These are found in (b) and (c) answer choices.

Conclusion

CONGRATULATIONS! You have made it this far because you have applied yourself diligently to practicing for the exam and no doubt improved your potential score considerably! Getting into a good school is a huge step in a journey that might be challenging at times but will be many times more rewarding and fulfilling. That is why being prepared is so important.

Good Luck!

Register for Free Updates and More Practice Test Questions

Register your purchase at https://www.test-preparation.ca/register/ for updates, free test tips and more practice test questions.

Visit us Online!

www.test-preparation.ca

https://www.facebook.com/CompleteTestPreparation/

https://www.youtube.com/user/MrTestPreparation

ONLINE RESOURCES

How to Prepare for a Test - The Ultimate Guide

https://www.test-preparation.ca/prepare-test/

Learning Styles - The Complete Guide

https://www.test-preparation.ca/learning-style/

Test Anxiety Secrets!

https://www.test-preparation.ca/test-anxiety/

Time Management on a Test

https://www.test-preparation.ca/time-management/

Flash Cards - The Complete Guide

https://www.test-preparation.ca/flash-cards/

Test Preparation Video Series

https://www.test-preparation.ca/test-video/

How to Memorize - The Complete Guide

https://www.test-preparation.ca/memorize/

Online Library of Student Tips and Strategies

https://www.test-preparation.ca/students-say/

www.ingramcontent.com/pod-product-compliance
Lightning Source LLC
Chambersburg PA
CBHW072151070526
44585CB00015B/1092